THE ACCIDENTAL STRATEGIST

LESSONS IN BUSINESS VALUE CREATION
FROM
AIR TRAFFIC CONTROL

GARY M PEARSON

To my amazing wife Maria, who has been my rock and my reality check—thank you for keeping me grounded (and occasionally sane). I love you and I am excited for another 23 years and hopefully more.

To the girls who give me endless inspiration and reasons to keep going, Miah, Lauren, Stephanie, Nikki, Shannon, and Carly, even if I sometimes wonder if you're just here for the free food and the advice that you then choose to ignore.

To everyone who supported me on this winding leadership journey—you know who you are, and so do I. And, of course, to those who didn't—thanks for the memorable life lessons. They were... character-building.

Contents

HOW TO READ THIS BOOK
The Five Story Concepts

"The Accidental Strategist" uses a unique blend of storytelling and real-world insights to guide readers through six essential value-creation topics. Each chapter includes an icon to assist you in quickly identifying its format.

Destinations

The value creation topics: Research & evaluation, Strategy, Culture, Urgency, Execution, and Discipline

Waypoints

The key learning points on the way to each destination.

Air Traffic Control

Real-world stories from air traffic control that teach us about value creation.

Personal Air Traffic Control Experiences

Lessons learned from my air traffic control experience.

Personal Business Learning Experiences

Stories and lessons learned from my business journey from a software tester to CEO.

Through relatable experiences from air traffic control and key learning points, this book offers a personal journey to mastering strategic thinking and value creation.

Who is the Accidental Strategist?

The Backstory

Most people go their entire lives without getting run over by a ship. I managed it twice.

The first time, I was seventeen and in Lagos, Nigeria. A crew member's wife had a suspected ruptured appendix, and we needed to get her to shore quickly. Our solution: the ship's lifeboat. Looking back, maybe we should have checked the engine more thoroughly.

We were deep in the port's entry channel when our engine made its grand exit. There was a thunderous bang, followed by a spray of oil that turned the air into a mechanical mist. Then silence. Dead in the water, as they say.

I'll never forget looking up to see a container ship looming over us, its bow rising like a steel cliff. In that moment, bobbing helplessly in one of Africa's busiest shipping lanes, I learned what true existential dread feels like.

I survived, obviously. But fate wasn't done with its maritime humor.

The second time, I wasn't even on the water. I was sitting at my desk in the shipyard office, doing paperwork, definitely not expecting to get run over by a ship while on dry land. But a captain, fresh from having his vessel painted, misjudged his turn. The ship's hull burst through my office wall.

As glass and debris rained down around my desk, I had to appreciate the irony. I'd survived being run over by a ship in the middle of a port entry channel, only to have one find me on land.

Some people collect stamps. I apparently collect near-death

experiences.

As a navigator on oil tankers, I experienced the Atlantic's finest storms up close and personal. Our supertanker would groan and bend with each towering wave. Every time the deck twisted, I wondered if today was the day we'd join Atlantis. Fortunately, the front didn't fall off. If you understand that reference, you are my kind of reader. If you don't understand, YouTube is your friend.

At 27, I joined the Royal Air Force as an officer and air traffic controller. The air force was outstanding at providing access to adventure. I nearly drowned kayaking in Germany, crash-landed in a hot-air balloon, and broke my back and several other bones paragliding in the French Alps. After a couple of surgeries and a few months of convalescing, I somehow convinced myself to return to paragliding. That was until I realized after jumping from a cliff, I was flying a shredded paraglider. Plummeting groundward, without steering, I had a heart-to-heart with myself. I decided I'd leave paragliding to those who enjoy gambling with gravity.

Next came my time working for a Ukrainian cargo airline. Flying on the Antonov 124, the world's largest plane, I racked up an impressive collection of aviation horror stories. An engine explosion during takeoff in Dubai, a 'landing' that left pieces of our undercarriage strewn across the runway in Khartoum, a major bird strike that took out an engine over Italy, and a takeoff in Sri Lanka, where we were dangerously over the maximum weight limit. Spoiler alert: we miraculously cleared the end of the runway and didn't become a news headline.

These adventures, spanning six countries I've called home and the eighty I've passed through, weren't just about adrenaline fixes. They were lessons in risk, decision-making under fire, and understanding why complex systems fail. Each incident, each split-second decision, and every narrow escape gave me an education in resilience that no classroom ever could.

Sitting in my office today, surrounded by business books and strategy frameworks, I can't help but smile at the path that led me here. If you had told me during my days in the air traffic control tower that I would eventually advise boards and CEOs on business strategy, I would have thought you were crazy.

The transition from the control tower to the boardroom wasn't smooth. When I first entered the corporate world, I felt like a fish out of water. The jargon was different; the stakes were lower (no lives at risk), and the pace felt maddeningly slow compared to the rapid-fire world of air traffic control or the split-second decisions required when things go wrong.

But as I navigated this unfamiliar terrain, the parallels became clear. The complex systems, the need for crystal-clear communication, and the importance of seeing both the big picture and the minute details were there in different forms. The chaos of business became as clear to me as a radar screen when I realized that each department was like an aircraft, each market a flight path, and each resource allocation as critical as managing precious airspace.

I wasn't an ex-air traffic controller in a business setting. I was a survivor, a risk manager, a systems thinker who had learned his trade not in business school but in the unforgiving classrooms of real-world chaos. My unique perspective, shaped by narrowly avoiding disaster across multiple continents and contexts, brought something different to the world of business strategy.

That's what led me to write this book. It's not just about business principles or strategy frameworks. It's about the wisdom from experiencing failure up close, understanding how systems break down, and about learning to navigate complexity in any context. It brings together lessons learned from maritime near-misses, aviation close calls, and the controlled chaos of air traffic control into a unique approach to business strategy.

Some might call me fortunate to have survived. I prefer to think of myself as fortunate, fortunate to have gained insights that few others have had the opportunity (or misfortune) to gain. This book is my way of sharing those insights, of showing how the most valuable thinking often comes from the unexpected places.

Welcome to the world of the Accidental Strategist.

CONTROLLED CHAOS

A True Story of Tragedy

The heat shimmered across the runway at Royal Air Force Gutersloh in West Germany. On the 20th of June 1989, Harrier XW925 roared into the sky. The late afternoon sortie tested the pilot's skill, precision, and mastery of a machine that defied gravity through brute force. With Gutersloh less than 100 miles from the East German Border, the Harrier force was a front-line deterrent against a possible Soviet invasion.

The Harrier pilot maneuvered the plane with the finesse that only comes from thousands of hours in the cockpit. Behind him, an Army Air Corps Captain and helicopter pilot on a ride along, new to the Harrier's peculiarities, sat wide-eyed, eager, and anxious.

The first part of the flight had been flawless. The Harrier sliced through the low and medium-level maneuvers, a testament to the pilot's ability and the rigorous training that had sculpted his instincts. This was what decades of military aviation experience demanded: reflexes honed to perfection, decisions made without hesitation, guided by procedures drilled into every flight, every briefing, every moment in the air.

The Harrier returned to the airfield, and the mission shifted. The pilot began practicing the unusual flight modes of the Harrier, short take-offs, and vertical landings. The day's sweltering heat had pushed the plane's capabilities to the edge. With water injection, a critical part for boosting thrust, almost depleted, the vertical landing maneuver was risky. Years of discipline dictated his every action. The pilot knew the operating limitations. He would attempt the landing and abort with precision if necessary.

Approaching the vertical landing pad, the pilot maneuvered the Harrier into a hover. The jet floated above the surface, suspended by its powerful thrust-vectoring nozzles. On the ground, the control tower watched. Every controller, every team member, was ready for what came next.

The Harrier hovered 100 feet above the metal vertical landing pad, but something was off. Tuned to the slightest deviation, the pilot felt the aircraft straining. The heat, the weight, and the lack of thrust were coming together in the wrong way. His decision to abort was swift, made in a split second. "Going around," he called over the radio, calm but urgent. The aircraft surged forward, but too slowly.

The right wing dipped; the nose lifted, a sign that things were going wrong fast. Inside the cockpit, alarms blared, and the pilot made the call. "Eject, Eject, Eject!"

The Army captain at once reacted, recalling the preflight briefing. His instincts kicked in, and he pulled the ejection handle; his seat blasted him out of the cockpit. But the pilot, focused on controlling the Harrier until the last second, delayed. In those moments, the Harrier dropped and hit the ground, skidding and cartwheeling towards the edge of the airfield and into the canal.

There was a distinct pop of the firing ejection seat. In the tower, we fell into our roles. Procedures took over. This was what we prepared for. Every emergency drill, every debriefing, had been for this moment.

The tower erupted into action, though it felt like a symphony of practiced movements. Each controller knew their place. The drills and past accidents had made it automatic. There was no hesitation or confusion. "State one, state one, state one," sounded over the station-wide broadcast, alerting the base that there was an emergency. "Harrier crashed near the Western Pad with two people on board. Both have ejected."

The emergency crew was already moving, vehicles racing towards the crash site. Each crew member had drilled this response countless times that it was second nature. The fire trucks and ambulances weaved through the airfield, reaching the wreckage with astonishing speed. The tower cleared the path for the rescue teams.

Controllers and assistants coordinated the emergency response inside the tower. We cleared the airspace of traffic to make sure the rescue operations proceeded unhindered. Radios crackled, and updates flew between the response teams, station operations, and the tower. The air traffic controllers never faltered. They didn't need to think about their next steps; they knew what to do and did it with unshakable focus.

At the crash site, the rescue team found the Army captain alive. His training had saved him. He ejected the instant he heard the command. His injuries were severe but survivable. The RAF pilot, though, had not made it. His ejection had come too late, firing him into nearby trees, the impact too violent. The moment's weight hit the rescue team, but even in their grief, their roles were clear. They worked efficiently and respectfully, knowing that every action still mattered.

In the tower, a somber silence descended. We continued our duties, but the loss weighed on us. Every action we had taken had been instinctive, each decision flowing into the next without hesitation.

Harrier XW925

An Opportunity to Learn

As the sun set on RAF Gutersloh that fateful June day in 1989, the aftermath of the Harrier crash left us with lessons that extend far beyond air traffic control.

No corporate challenge ever equates to the immense grief of losing lives. When applied to business contexts, the lessons drawn from this heartrending event drive meaningful improvements while considering the original tragedy's profound human toll.

Each team member had a defined role and executed it when a crisis struck. From the controller's split-second decision-making to the coordinated actions of the emergency response crew, we saw the importance of organizational structure and well-defined responsibilities.

The radio traffic between the tower and rescue teams mirrored communication channels in any organization. In times of crisis, as in times of opportunity, moving information either empowers or hinders a company's response.

The team's rigorous training highlights the need for investing in people. As we perfected our skills through countless drills and simulations, businesses must cultivate talent and offer continuous learning opportunities to prepare for everyday operations and unforeseen challenges.

Perhaps more striking was the disciplined execution. Faced with tragedy, there was no panic, no confusion, only a focused, procedural response. This unwavering commitment to established protocols, even under extreme pressure, is a testament to strong organizational culture and consistency in execution.

Yet, amidst the precision and professionalism, we were reminded of the human element. The lost life that day weighed on us, underscoring the consequences of our actions and decisions. In business, as in life, we must never lose sight of the human impact of our choices.

As we reflected on the events, we recognized that our ability to respond to crises was not born overnight. It resulted from years of strategic planning, experience, continuous learning and improvement, organizational development, and a relentless commitment to excellence. These qualities create cultures that separate thriving businesses from those that falter when faced with adversity.

The tragedy at RAF Gutersloh taught us that success and sometimes survival hinges on our ability to prepare, adapt, and execute. Whether in an air traffic control tower or a corporate boardroom, the principles stay the same: simple strategy, strong organization, open communication, invested people, and disciplined execution are the foundations of resilience and success.

THE UNSEEN WEB OF AVIATION SAFETY

Putting Ego Aside

Throughout this book, you will read stories of air traffic control and crisis management. The stories highlight the role of air traffic controllers in maintaining safety in our skies, but painting controllers as lone heroes is a disservice to the aviation community.

The intention is not to elevate air traffic controllers above other aviation professionals, but to illuminate the system within which they work. I put my air traffic controller ego aside to acknowledge that every crisis averted, every safe landing under challenging conditions, and every smooth day of operations results from a complex, interconnected team effort.

Air traffic controllers are one crucial link in a larger chain. Without the dedicated work of countless other professionals, the aviation system as we know it does not work.

Several of the aviation stories resulted in a loss of life. I do not intend to equate tragedy and loss of life with business failures. I have attempted to treat the loss of life with dignity and respect.

As you read the accounts in this book, I encourage you to consider the broader context of each situation. While the spotlight often falls on the controller's actions, behind each decision is a network of professionals working in concert to guide planes with precision, unnoticed by those below.

The stories are a testament to the skill and dedication of air traffic controllers and the remarkable synergy of the larger aviation ecosystem. This collective effort, this unseen web of ability and cooperation, keeps our skies safe.

Navigating A Business

With Air Traffic Control Precision

Have you ever wondered what air traffic control and businesses have in common? More than you think. As someone who's spent time in both the control tower and the boardroom, the view isn't too different, if you know how to look.

What on earth does controlling planes have to do with my business? That's where you're in for a surprise. Air traffic controllers aren't the unsung heroes of aviation; they're the secret to business success that you never knew existed.

Think about it. These aviation specialists are juggling lives, multi-million dollar machines, and split-second decisions with a cool that makes James Bond jealous. But they don't confine their ability to an ivory control tower. It's a treasure trove of wisdom waiting to be unleashed in the business world.

Let's take a whirlwind tour. An air traffic controller's ability extends far beyond guiding planes:

The Project Management Office: Coordinating resources, managing risks, and ensuring smooth operations, sound familiar, business leaders?

The Stock Exchange Floor Managers: Orchestrating transactions in a high-stakes, fast-paced environment where split-second decisions make or break success.

The Supply Chain Specialists: Ensuring smooth flow, preventing bottlenecks, and optimizing routes, but with planes instead of products.

The Cybersecurity Operations Center: Monitoring, identifying potential threats, and coordinating rapid responses to ensure safety and continuity.

The Crisis Management Team: Always prepared, always alert, handling the unexpected with calm efficiency and strategic thinking.

The Executive Assistants: Juggling multiple priorities, managing schedules, and ensuring everything runs seamlessly for the 'bosses,' the pilots, passengers, and airlines.

The Global Logistics Department: Managing complex international movements, navigating regulations, and ensuring smooth operations across borders.

The Orchestra Conductors: Bringing together diverse elements, ensuring harmony, and creating a symphony of safe and efficient air travel.

In the following chapters, we'll explore how applying the principles and practices of air traffic control creates extraordinary value in business.

This book will explore how to boost your business value-creation efforts and transform your business strategy and execution using a framework called ReSCUED:

Research and evaluation

Strategy

Culture

Urgency

Execution

Discipline.

You might be thinking, "Great, another business acronym." Stick with me. Whether you're a CEO steering your company through turbulent markets or a manager optimizing your team's performance, the principles we'll explore here help you navigate the complex airspace of modern business.

As we examine each part of the ReSCUED framework, we'll draw parallels between the world of air traffic control and the dynamic landscape of business. Air traffic controllers must watch, adjust, and optimize; business leaders must navigate their organizations through complex and ever-changing circumstances.

Throughout this book, we'll explore how the applied principles that keep our skies safe keep your business soaring. From managing multiple moving parts and making split-second decisions to maintaining communication and expecting potential conflicts, the lessons from air traffic control apply to the business world.

Each section, called a destination, will introduce a part of the ReSCUED framework, explaining its relevance to business value creation, strategy, and execution. We'll then illustrate these concepts with real-world examples of air traffic control and business, demonstrating how the principles that guide planes through crowded airspace guide your company to success.

We're about to embark on a journey that will transform how you think about leading a business. And who knows? By the end, you will look at the sky and your company in a new way.

Value!

What is It?

Businesses do one thing: they exchange value. Value sits at the heart of an organization, whether they're chasing profits or pursuing a mission. But value depends on perspective.

Your company is a customer and a vendor. As a customer, the flow of your company value is outward. You exchange cash for the goods and services offered by the people you hire and the vendors you choose. Why do that? You need what they offer to exchange your goods and services with your customers, creating an inbound flow of value, i.e., what you receive for the goods and services you sell. The difference between inbound and outbound flows is profit (or loss). It also drives cash flow.

What is the point of this perpetual back-and-forth? You aim to maximize the ultimate exchange of value, the exchange of company ownership. The ultimate exchange is either partial, the exchange of shares, or complete, the acquisition of your company.

Private Equity is the perfect example of the ultimate exchange of value.

Private equity (PE) firms have a mission: acquire companies, enhance their value, and sell them at a profit. These firms invest capital into private companies or take public companies private to improve their performance, increase their value, and offer returns to their investors. These firms use various methods to assign value to a company. One common approach is to compare it with similar companies in the same industry, using financial metrics to show a valuation benchmark. They look at recent sales of comparable businesses to understand what buyers have been willing to pay in the market.

Another technique involves forecasting the company's future

cash flow and calculating its present value. For deals involving debt, private equity firms use models that assess how much to borrow and still meet their target returns. They will apply earnings multiples to show market trends or value companies based on their physical assets.

Strategic value is also important. Firms consider whether the acquisition will bring synergies or competitive advantages to their portfolio. External factors, such as the broader economy or market conditions, influence the final valuation.

Don't get caught up in the details here, but don't dismiss these fundamentals because you have grander plans. Do you dream of building a legacy to pass on to your family? Even this legacy is only realistic if you create value.

I asked several prominent private equity professionals what they sought in a company that makes it an acquisition candidate. A few things drive value. These factors aren't boxes to check. They're the core of determining if a company is worth PE time and money. Here's what they said matters to them:

"If your company isn't growing its revenue, we're not interested. Consistent, solid revenue growth tells us there's demand and that you're grabbing more of the market. Sustained growth is the minimum if you expand into new markets."

"It's about profits. Revenue is significant, but we care how much you keep. High EBITDA and strong margins show you've mastered efficiency. You're controlling costs, scaling up, and making it work."

"We're looking for companies with something special, a moat, a killer product, loyal customers, or technology that makes competitors sweat. You're in shape if you've got a solid position and barriers to entry."

"Run lean and scale fast. If you grow without ballooning costs, you've got our attention. Streamlining, cutting waste, and making every dollar work harder is value."

"Predictable, strong cash flow reduces debt and funds for future growth. If you're throwing off reliable free cash flow, you've got flexibility, and that's a major plus when considering investing."

"We invest not only in companies. We invest in people. A strong, experienced management team that's been through it, that's worth a premium. We're confident in the investment if the leadership knows how to execute."

"Is the market big enough? Is it growing? If you're in a large, expanding market with room to capture more share, that's a serious value driver. We want companies that are positioned to take advantage of that growth."

"A diverse, loyal customer base is gold. If you depend on a few key clients, that's a red flag. Recurring revenue and a broad base of customers reduce risk and add stability."

"Scalability is the secret sauce. If your business model lets you grow revenue without costs going through the roof, then you're primed for big returns. Tech platforms, standardized processes, anything that lets you scale fast matters."

"You can't ignore the big picture. We look at the trends shaping your industry, technology shifts, regulatory changes, and consumer behaviors. You're more valuable if you're in tune with the winds of change."

"PE firms love synergies. Whether it's cross-selling opportunities, cost-cutting across businesses, or operational efficiencies, we look for ways your company strengthens our portfolio."

"How much debt are you carrying, and can you handle it? Stacking the deal with leverage means carefully placing every dollar with a capital structure that keeps the ship steady, no matter how heavy the load. The ability to restructure and free up cash flow adds serious value."

"We're thinking about the exit. Whether it's an IPO, selling to a strategic buyer, or another PE firm, we want lucrative paths to cashing out. The smoother the exit, the better the valuation."

Let's distill these insights into four value-added objectives.

1. Improved Gross Margins

2. Managed Cash Flow

3. Mergers and Acquisitions

4. Revenue Growth

These drivers work together to shape the overall value. Nail several of these, and you're in a prominent position to attract serious interest and command a strong valuation. That's the game.

ReSCUED, What Will I Learn? A Framework for Navigating Complexity

A Framework for Navigating Complexity

Businesses live and die by the value they create. That value translates into revenue, profitability, and long-term sustainability. Yet, far too often, businesses focus on the wrong end of the equation. They chase revenue without asking why it isn't translating into profit or scale. They fight fires instead of addressing root causes.

A structured approach to value creation that starts where most business problems end: the bottom line.

ReSCUED is a practical, step-by-step process for diagnosing your business challenges and uncovering what drives value. But there's a twist: instead of starting with revenue or growth goals, ReSCUED works backward from your biggest pain points.

Before you can apply improvements, you need to understand where the problems lie. It's tempting to jump straight into fixing what seems broken, whether it's cutting costs, revamping a product, or boosting sales. Without identifying the true source of the issue, you risk wasting time and resources on superficial solutions. That's why the ReSCUED framework starts at the end: the bottom line. By analyzing your profits (or lack thereof), you gain a clear view of the symptoms, which allows you to trace them back to their root causes. This backward approach ensures that you address the actual problems, not just their surface-level manifestations, setting the stage for meaningful and lasting improvements.

Start at the End

Let's begin where the problems are most visible: your bottom line.

If your profits are poor or you're losing money, the immediate assumption might be that you need more revenue. But revenue isn't the root of the issue. Your bottom line is the difference between your margin contributions and your overhead costs (G&A). If you are losing money, your overheads are consuming too much of your gross margins.

Solution: Reduce overheads or increase margin contribution. Simple, right? Not quite. To fix profit, we need to dig deeper.

Reduce Overheads

Reducing overheads is about cutting excess costs while preserving what drives value in your business. Start by auditing your expenses to identify waste, then look for opportunities. The key is to streamline operations without compromising essential functions, making your business leaner, more efficient, and more focused on growth.

If your overheads are as optimal as they can be, then look at margin contributions.

Improving Margin Contribution

Margins are the cushion between your cost of goods sold and your revenue. To improve them, you can:

- Reduce the cost of goods sold (COGS): improve productivity and efficiency and reduce direct costs.

- Increase revenue: Boost sales without proportionately increasing costs.

How to Reduce the Cost of Goods Sold

Cutting costs isn't just about slashing budgets. It's about working smarter and increasing productivity and efficiency and reducing direct costs.

Reducing Direct Costs

Reducing direct costs is a key strategy for lowering your Cost of Goods Sold (COGS) and enhancing profitability. Direct costs are expenses directly tied to the production of your goods or services—such as raw materials, direct labor, and manufacturing supplies. By minimizing these costs, you can reduce COGS without sacrificing quality.

Improving Productivity and Efficiency

To reduce COGS and improve margins, your teams and processes need to be operating at peak efficiency. You can't achieve productivity by working harder;

Solution: Focus on execution.

Execution: The Bridge Between Strategy and Results

Execution is where strategy turns into action, or falls apart. Poor execution is often the silent killer of productivity, wasting time, money, and resources. Productivity is an output from execution. Productivity is driven by a high performance culture.

Developing a Culture of High Performance

Execution thrives in an environment where people feel motivated, processes are streamlined, and goals are aligned. In other words, you need a high-performance culture.

But what does a high-performance culture look like? It's not about endless hustle or flashy perks. It's about engagement, clarity, and alignment.

Building a High-Performance Culture

Two pillars build a strong culture.

1. Employee Engagement

2. Effective and Optimized Processes

Improving Employee Engagement

Engaged employees aren't just clocking in; they're invested in the company's success. But engagement doesn't happen by accident. According to Daniel Pink's *Drive*, true engagement comes from three elements:

- **Purpose**: Employees need to understand how their work contributes to something bigger.

- **Autonomy**: Give people the freedom to decide within their role.

- **Mastery**: Provide opportunities to learn, grow, and excel.

Improving Processes

Broken processes will cause even the most engaged employees to struggle. This is where systems thinking , the theory of constraints and discipline, come into play:

- **Systems Thinking**: Understand how all parts of the business interact and   influence one another.

- **Theory of Constraints**: Identify and address bottlenecks that slow down   productivity.

- **Discipline**: Discipline is the backbone of effective execution and continuous   improvement. It ensures that plans aren't just created, but followed   through with consistency and accountability. In execution, discipline means sticking to priorities, maintaining focus, and avoiding distractions   that derail progress.

Turning Attention to Revenue

You've optimized costs, productivity, and culture. Now it's time to focus on growing revenue. Revenue growth comes from two places:

1. **Broadening your addressable market**: Find new customers or markets to serve.

2. **Improving market share**: Attract more customers in your

current market.

But growing revenue requires more than wishful thinking.

Broadening Addressable Markets

To broaden the market, solve more customer Problems. Every successful business starts by solving a problem. The better you understand your customers' pain points, the more value you can deliver.

Increasing Market Share

To increase market share you must find more prospects and close more deals. If you're struggling to increase market share, the issue lies in client retention and acquisition. Keeping existing customers is essential for stability, while acquiring new ones drives growth. If either is faltering, it's a sign that your customer experience might need improvement, or your marketing and sales strategies aren't resonating. To find more customers and close more deals requires that you differentiate your solutions from those of your competitors.

Differentiating

To stand out, you need to offer something unique, something that sets you apart from competitors and resonates with your customers. Differentiation can take many forms: a superior product, exceptional customer service, innovative features, or even a compelling brand story. It's not just about being different for the sake of it; your uniqueness must solve a real customer problem or fulfill a need better than anyone else.

Build a Strategy

Strategy ties everything together. It's the roadmap that defines where you're going and how you'll get there. Without it, even the best intentions will drift aimlessly.

The ReSCUED Framework in Action

What makes ReSCUED so effective is its simplicity. Instead of overwhelming you with dozens of priorities, it focuses on six interconnected drivers of value:

1. **Research & Evaluation**: Lay the groundwork with insights and analysis.

2. **Strategy**: Define your direction and competitive edge.

3. **Culture**: Build an engaged, high-performing team.

4. **Urgency**: Prioritize and act with focus.

5. **Execution**: Turn plans into results.

6. **Discipline**: Maintain consistency and accountability.

Each step builds on the previous one, creating a cycle of continuous improvement.

Why does ReSCUED Work?

The beauty of ReSCUED is that it shifts the focus to causes, not symptoms. If you're struggling with profits, the answer isn't to throw more money at marketing. If productivity is low, the answer isn't to demand longer hours.

Before you work forward, work backward to uncover the proper drivers of value. Don't just about fix what's broken; build a business that thrives, one step at a time.

The ReSCUED framework isn't a magic wand, but it is a proven method for creating value. Whether your challenge is poor margins, disengaged employees, or stagnant revenue, ReSCUED gives you a clear path forward.

Start where you are. Focus on one area at a time. And remember, real value isn't just about the numbers, it's about creating a business that works for the long haul.

That's the power of ReSCUED. It's your roadmap to sustainable growth and success.

BECOMING THE ACCIDENTAL STRATEGIST

From Air Traffic Control to the C-Suite

"Pearson, get in here!" came the shout from the office next door. I knew from experience what it meant. The CEO wanted to share his ideas, thoughts, or feelings. Undoubtedly, it meant more work for me.

Our company was a maze of competing interests, conflicting systems, and unrealized potential. I had watched our core products tread water. Our EBITDA swung between profit and loss like a pendulum, with no discernible rhythm. I took part in several misses, where investments in new products failed.

The CEO believed in internal competition. "Let the best business unit win," he often said, his eyes gleaming with the excitement of a gambler at a roulette table. But, our matrix management hamstrung his vision, leaving our business unit VPs with grand plans but no authority over the resources they needed to execute those plans.

The CEO's answer to missed revenue targets was straightforward: bring more players onto the field, and sheer numbers will turn the tide. New business units sprouted, each promising to be the key to unlocking our growth. But instead of a thriving ecosystem, we had created a jungle where each unit fought for survival, often at the expense of others. Something had to give. Still, I didn't suspect what came next.

In a moment of clarity (or desperation), he said. "We need to fix stuff," usual bravado replaced by a weary sigh. "And by we, I mean you. You are now the COO; get to it." Promoted from vice president to chief operating officer without warning, unprepared and facing a vague mandate, I stepped into a new role. Fix stuff, two words that defined the next chapter of my career.

Baby Steps

Fight or Flight

I felt like a junior air traffic control officer looking at the radar screen for the first time. Hundreds of tracks heading in random directions without an obvious method or purpose.

As I settled into my new role as COO, I realized it was a blessing and a curse. I now had authority over the business units and almost unchecked power to make changes. But with that power came the weight of responsibility. Our company's future rested on my ability to untangle the Gordian knot of our operations.

The irony didn't escape my notice. Here I was, tasked with crafting a rescue plan-without being told so, for a company running in competitive chaos (an environment where my ATC experience helped me thrive). I didn't truly understand what strategy meant. What I had was a firm grasp of operations management. I had a talent for understanding the big picture and the foresight to see how changes to the little picture affected our future state. It wasn't much, but it was a start.

I began by mapping out our current state: six business units, resources stretched thin, duplicated efforts, and a need for unified direction.

We culled non-contributing business units and eliminated several executive positions.

Our core product, once stagnant, found new life as we reallocated resources to innovation. We identified complementary services that augmented our primary offering, creating more revenue streams without requiring new business units.

The change was like the difference between controlling traffic around multiple closely situated airports and controlling traffic around one or two airports separated by many miles. Procedures were simpler. The bigger picture was less crowded, and the organization had space to optimize its operations. Insights surfaced, and the once cutthroat scramble for resources softened, leaving more room for collaboration than competition.

As we worked through the changes, something happened. The fog of internal competition lifted, revealing a clearer vision of our company.

The EBITDA pendulum slowed its wild swings, settling into a more predictable rhythm. We were surviving, and we were making money.

So, all's well that ends well! Not quite.

I smile, looking back. The boss tasked me with "fixing stuff." It wasn't the path I had expected to take, but it led the company far beyond what I had imagined.

As the months passed, I started seeing the old signs of problems. We went from initiative to initiative and solved one problem after another. There was an inconsistency in what we were doing. Some months were fantastic, and others not so much. We did not have a long-term plan or strategy.

I understood the intricate dance of operations, resources, and market demands. But, my professional development required me to know more. I recognized that to succeed, I needed to develop an environment where every part of the company worked towards a common goal.

No longer the operations guy, I had become the accidental strategist, ready for whatever challenge came next.

Big Picture, Little Picture

Connecting the Pieces

Air traffic controllers have one skill that stands out. Controllers excel at distilling complex dynamic situations into smaller chunks.

Let's use this skill and analyze a business using an elementary example.

You decide to open a business, and you want to sell pies. Your friends and family tell you your pies are delicious. You thought of a cool name and have a logo designed. Like many startups, it's more of a hobby at this stage. But, if your pies are as good as your friends tell you, the day will come when you have to transition from a hobby to a disciplined company.

You have a dream. One day, you will own pie shops in every town in your country, and they will sell world championship-winning pies - **your vision**.

You will sell Apple Pies to independent retail bakers - **your mission**.

Because you make the tastiest pies, there is more demand for them than for your competitors' pies. Your pies are more profitable to the store because your distribution network is consistent and fast, minimizing the bakery's cost and effort to manage its stock - **your value proposition**.

You will sell 100 units a month by the end of the first year and, by the end-of-year three, 1000 a month. You will add three more pie types in the same period - **your goals**.

The company will only use locally sourced organic ingredients - **your values**.

You source ingredients from approved vendors. An in-house baker prepares the ingredients. The oven manager bakes them. The packaging team packs them. You sell through direct sales. The pies are delivered by the internal logistics team - **your system**.

You store frozen ingredients at 25 degrees Fahrenheit, fresh ingredients at 40 degrees. The bakers will follow the company's secret apple pie recipe. Customers are invoiced on the first of each month - **your processes**.

Commercial ovens, refrigerators, freezers, utensils, pots, pans, mixing bowls, and oven gloves - **your tools**.

Pies are prepared and shipped to the retailers from a central bakery - **your infrastructure**.

There is a strong demand for gluten-free pies. You have interest from supermarket chains. You will sell specialist pies to a growing market and expand your distribution network - **your strategy**.

You want to improve your profit margins and source cheaper ingredients - **a tactical initiative**.

So, what is the point of this example? These definitions guide the things you need to do to create value.

Your objectives are to decrease the resources you use (the input) and maximize the value of the goods and services you sell (the output). Reducing the time from input to output will help your cash position, and as we know, cash is king. So, how does the baker analogy help to do that?

Vision and mission drive employee performance. More pies are baked and delivered in less time with fewer people, lowering costs and improving cash flow.

The value proposition improves market share, adding more customers and increasing profits.

The goals set targets, adding discipline and focus and improving productivity.

Your values drive employee behavior, customer loyalty, and engagement, increasing sales.

Your tool choices impact cost and productivity. The first oven bakes 24 pies in one hour instead of 12 for the second oven. The automatic pie-packing equipment increases operational efficiency. Both impact cost and cash generation by reducing the time from order to payment.

Your infrastructure has the same impact. A central bakery and distribution center costs less than multiple national bakeries and distribution centers.

Your strategy of selling gluten-free pies increases demand and improves the value proposition for your customers, the independent bakers. The supermarkets boost demand for your products.

Buying cheaper ingredients reduces costs and increases gross margins and profits.

This book describes an approach to increasing the output while reducing the input. You will learn how to think holistically. Buying cheaper ingredients helps with margins, but how does the new pie taste, and how does it influence the end customer demand? Larger ovens improve the tools but add costs, affecting capital expenditure, cash flow, and cash. You will learn to think of the big picture and the little picture, the strategy, and the execution.

THINKING

One, Two and Three-Dimensional

What makes someone suitable to be an air traffic controller? A company from New Zealand created a tool for assessing the likelihood that a candidate will graduate from ATC College and succeed in the operational training phase.

The company took a different approach to this challenging task; "We don't focus on what makes someone good at air traffic control; we focus on the traits that will make them a bad one." Visualizing airspace in three dimensions was fundamental to the role. You either can or cannot. It is not a learned skill. If you cannot, you will flunk out or be a stressed controller who lives on the edge.

As a CEO, you must visualize the organization in three dimensions and understand the relationship between your decisions and outcomes, and the impact of external and internal forces. Three-dimensional thinking separates competent leaders from those who struggle to navigate the complex, interconnected business landscape. It's a skill to be developed and a fundamental mindset that must be ingrained in how leaders approach every decision and challenge.

What distinguishes three-dimensional thinking from one and two dimensions?

One-dimensional thinking

One-dimensional thinking is approaching a problem and looking for a solution.

For example, when sales decline, many businesses come quickly to the conclusion that they need to reach more customers. The assumption is that increasing brand exposure through a bigger marketing budget, more extensive ad campaigns, new digital marketing strategies, and more aggressive promotions will drive more traffic to their store or website, boosting sales.

This solution leads to more eyes on the product, translating to more purchases. However, while it often addresses one aspect of the equation, it doesn't resolve the sales decline's root cause.

Two-dimensional Thinking

Two-dimensional thinking looks at potential alternatives. The two-dimensional thinker investigates the data before deciding what to do next.

Instead of bringing in more customers, the company focuses on improving the customers' experience. Are customers facing long checkout times? Is the website difficult to navigate, or are employees trained? A poor shopping experience leads to customer attrition regardless of your marketing.

Are declining sales a problem of visibility or experience? Sometimes, the issue lies in pricing strategy or inventory management. A more nuanced approach might involve conducting a detailed analysis of their product pricing relative to competitors and customer expectations. Is the store overstocked on low-demand items and understocked on high-demand ones? Are they pricing items to drive customers to buy from competitors?

Three-dimensional Thinking

Three-dimensional thinking is summarized with a question. Who or what does this decision impact?

Let's revisit the earlier example, Optimize Customer Experience. The company focuses on improving the in-store or online shopping experience.

Who or what is affected?

Internal Stakeholders:

Customer Service & Sales Staff: Streamlining the shopping process, improving store layouts, or providing customer service training impacts employees. Enhanced service expectations raise stress levels unless managed.

Operations & IT: If optimizing customer experience involves updates in technology (like implementing faster check-out processes or website redesigns), it will disrupt during the upgrade. IT teams will face added workloads and troubleshooting challenges.

External Stakeholders:

Customers: A better shopping experience will increase satisfaction and brand loyalty and create positive word-of-mouth recommendations. But changes to familiar processes or interfaces frustrate existing customers if not rolled out with caution.

Contractors/Vendors: If better customer experience means redesigning stores or updating technology, this creates external dependencies on contractors or third-party vendors, whose quality and timeliness of work impact the business.

By considering who and what is affected, the business avoids creating friction with employees or alienating its loyal customer base through abrupt changes that aren't well-communicated.

Thinking in three dimensions is a valuable skill, and it's a necessity. Like the example of air traffic controller selection in New Zealand, where the focus was on identifying traits that make someone unsuitable for the role, we apply a similar principle to business leadership.

A leader must be able to visualize their organization in multiple dimensions. This includes understanding the intricate relationships between decisions and their ripple effects across various stakeholders and business functions.

Identifying a problem and implementing the most evident solution is not enough (one-dimensional thinking). Two-dimensional thinking, which considers alternatives, is better but still falls short. Decision-making at a leadership level requires three-dimensional thinking: the ability to anticipate and consider the broader impacts of decisions on internal and external stakeholders.

Leaders who cannot think in three dimensions, like an air traffic controller who can't visualize airspace, live on the edge of disaster. They solve immediate problems but create new ones or miss opportunities for synergistic solutions.

In business, the inability to think in three dimensions leads to:

1. Unintended consequences that negate the benefits of decisions

2. Damaged relationships with key stakeholders

3. Missed opportunities for holistic solutions

4. Increased organizational stress and conflict

5. Reduced long-term sustainability and resilience

It's as much about avoiding foreseeable errors as making wise decisions by adopting a broader perspective.

Decision-Making

How Choices Dictate Future States

In quantum physics, there's a fascinating concept called the many-worlds interpretation, suggesting that every time a decision is made at the quantum level, the universe splits into multiple realities, each following a different path based on that decision.

These parallel business universes unfold based on the choices made at critical junctures. The marketing strategy you choose, the people you hire, the products you develop, each decision point is a nexus of potential realities, branching out into an infinite web of possibilities.

The system will not work for you if you cannot master the skill of decision-making. Making decisions is at the heart of leadership and organizational success. Business leaders face endless choices and make decisions that will dictate the fate of their organizations. Decisions that range from daily operational choices to long-term moves that shape the company's future.

Even amidst uncertainty or pressure, sound judgment skills allow leaders to guide their organizations through challenges and opportunities. They inspire confidence in their teams, stakeholders, and customers, creating positive organizational outcomes.

Learning to decide is the first step in everything we do in value creation. A novice air traffic controller must master the basics before handling complexity; aspiring leaders must first understand the principles and processes of decision-making.

This foundational knowledge is making choices and understanding how to approach decisions, what factors to consider, and how to evaluate outcomes. By focusing on this essential skill, leaders develop the confidence and competence to guide their organizations through calm and turbulent skies.

Imagine the air traffic control radar as a display of the present and a dynamic map of potential futures. Every action a controller takes, directing a plane to climb or change heading, alters the trajectory of that flight and the surrounding flights. A proactive controller must anticipate these changes, evaluating multiple scenarios before giving instructions.

This involves real-time analysis of several potential solutions. Each decision opens a distinct set of future states with associated risks and benefits. It's like nudging a single atom in a crowded particle collider. Just as that tiny shift causes a chain reaction of collisions, altering the course of one plane triggers a ripple effect across the entire sky. Other planes must change their heading, and the airspace becomes dynamic and chaotic, where every movement influences the next. In both scenarios, a single decision cascades into complex, unpredictable outcomes, requiring constant vigilance and precise control to manage the chaos.

The controller must weigh these choices against the current state, considering the weather, air traffic density, aircraft speed, altitude, and potential conflicts with other planes.

Each choice leads to a different future state. The controller must consider each decision's outcome and downstream effects. Will the alternative route or altitude bring the plane into conflict with another further along its path? What impact will this decision have on overall airspace efficiency?

Proactive controllers excel because they don't react to what's before them. They project into the future, visualizing how their decisions will shape the minutes and hours to come. This forward-thinking approach keeps air traffic flowing even in the busiest skies.

Every decision you make sets the organization on a fresh path. Whether entering a new market, launching a product, or restructuring a department, each choice opens a different future state with challenges and opportunities.

Business leaders need the ability to visualize these futures, weighing the probable outcomes of each decision before acting.

This requires a deep understanding of the business's current state and a forward-looking mindset that expects changes in the market, customer behavior, and competitive landscape.

Proactive business leaders react to the present, but they shape the future. They consider multiple scenarios, analyze the potential risks and rewards, and choose the path that best aligns with the organization's long-term aspirations. This ability to foresee the implications of today's decisions and navigate the complexities of tomorrow sets successful leaders apart.

But you cannot expect to make the right choices every time; changing course is not a badge of shame. Faced with evidence that shows you made a mistake, revising your choices is a hallmark of leadership and sound decision-making. Recognizing when a choice is no longer optimal and having the courage to pivot is essential.

However, reversing courses creates its own set of turbulence and challenges.

Changing direction will lead to resistance, especially if stakeholders have invested time, resources, or emotional energy into the original plan. Share the reasons for change and address concerns. It helps to foster trust and cooperation in the new direction.

Reversing course often leads to delays and disruptions, as resources need to be reallocated, timelines adjusted, and new plans formulated.

The very act of changing direction can erode confidence among team members, customers, and partners. Acknowledge the shift, communicate the revised approach, and show a renewed commitment to the new path forward. The decision to change course has financial ramifications, as the costs incurred in the earlier direction are sometimes not recoverable.

Despite these drawbacks, changing course when necessary is vital. The key lies in balancing adaptability and decisiveness. Thorough analysis and consideration of potential consequences are essential for making informed decisions about when and how to change direction. Leaders must navigate the complexities of change by understanding the forces at play. Recognizing the potential downsides of reversing course while embracing adaptability allows leaders to make adjustments confidently, minimizing disruption and maximizing the chances of achieving desired outcomes.

Seven Tips for Better Decision-Making

An Air Traffic Control Approach

Air traffic controllers continually evaluate the current state by asking themselves, "What do I do if this happens?" And the reverse, "What happens if I do this?" They consider several solutions, readying themselves to act if the what-if became real. There are reasons a controller's thinking never stops.

1. Early detection of a problem often presents multiple solutions.

2. Late detection of a problem reduces the number of solutions, and the solutions you are left with likely need more extreme actions.

3. Details are essential, but consider the bigger picture. Making isolated choices is poor practice. Businesses are complex, with endless interconnected pieces.

4. The information you gather is noise mixed with valuable data. Decision-making is easier if you learn to separate and discard the noise.

5. Multitasking does not exist, but time slicing does. Those who synthesize and prioritize craft effective solutions.

6. The quality of information is more valuable than the quantity. Don't overwhelm yourself with unnecessary data and excessive analysis.

7. Learn to use your team. Even in air traffic control, group decisions are routine.

You may have the luxury of dealing with one problem at a time, but it's atypical. My experience is of multiple simultaneous problems, often wrapped up in a crisis. How did I handle it? I did as every controller does; I eliminated noise and prioritized. Priority is determined by two factors: what is the severity of the problem, and how fast is the problem moving? To be more exact, how much time do I have before the impact is irreversible and new problems occur? This is where you need to use judgment.

Is the lack of a decision that will cause a severe impact a priority over one that results in lesser consequences? It suggests dealing with the dangerous consequences first. If the bigger problem moves slower, do you have time to resolve the lesser issue first? There is no hard and fast rule here. Your business circumstances determine the priority.

Decisions are not only required to solve problems but also to capitalize on opportunities. Unlike problems, which seldom disappear if you ignore them, opportunities do. Keep this in mind as you prioritize your actions and choices. Again, it's where judgment, not rules, helps. What is the potential damage from an unresolved problem compared with the long-term benefits of an opportunity?

INTUITION

It's Real, and It's Spectacular

You're staring at your computer screen, surrounded by stacks of reports, financial projections, and market analysis. Your inbox is overflowing with opinions from your team, and your phone won't stop buzzing with urgent requests. You know you need to decide, and fast. But the more data you gather, the harder it becomes to choose a path forward. Welcome to the world of paralysis analysis, where abundant information becomes your worst enemy.

As a business leader, you've likely experienced being trapped in this decision-making quicksand. The fear of making the wrong choice keeps you frozen, analyzing and re-analyzing data. Meanwhile, opportunities slip away, and problems compound. You're not alone in this struggle. In today's data-driven world, paralysis analysis has become an epidemic among business leaders.

But what if there was a way to break free from this paralysis? What if you develop the ability to make swift and confident decisions, even when faced with complex information and high stakes?

You are standing in front of two doors. Behind one lies success, and behind the other, failure. You have mere seconds to choose. Your palms are sweaty, your heart races. Which door do you pick? Business leaders often come across similar decisions. The pressure is on, and the clock is ticking. How do you make the right call?

Enter Malcolm Gladwell and his groundbreaking book, "Blink: The Power of Thinking Without Thinking." Gladwell invites us into a world where decisions are made in the blink of an eye. Intuition trumps analysis, and our unconscious mind is the unsung hero of decision-making. But what does this mean for you, the business leader, navigating the tumultuous waters of corporate decision-making?

Let's start with 'thin-slicing.' You are at a bustling farmers' market faced with mountains of produce. Each pile claims to be the freshest and most delicious. How do you choose? Without realizing it, your brain is thin-slicing, taking thin slices of experience and using them to make rapid judgments. That slight discoloration on the tomato? Your brain notices it before you do. The subtle aroma of ripe peaches? Your unconscious is processing it. This is your adaptive unconscious at work, sifting through a sea of information to help you make lightning-fast decisions.

Now, imagine this scenario happening in your boardroom. You're presented with stacks of reports, endless spreadsheets, and a chorus of opinions from your team. Your conscious mind feels overwhelmed, but your adaptive unconscious is at work, piecing together patterns and insights from your years of experience. This is thin-slicing in action.

This rapid cognition isn't infallible. Just as a skilled art forger can fool the most discerning eye, our snap judgments sometimes lead us astray. Gladwell calls this the "dark side of blink." It's what happens when our unconscious biases hijack our decision-making. Remember the last time you hired someone because they "felt right," only to realize later they were a poor fit? That's the dark side of blink at work.

This is where the 'Warren Harding Error' comes into play. Warren Harding, often considered one of the least effective U.S. presidents, was elected in part because he looked presidential. It reminds us how easily superficial qualities sway us. You need to guard against this error. The charismatic job candidate, the flashy new technology, and the foolproof business plan can trigger our snap judgments. The challenge is to recognize when to trust these judgments and when to dig deeper.

But don't think for a moment that Gladwell is advocating for the death of deliberate thinking. Far from it. The real magic happens when you learn to balance intuitive and analytical thinking.

So, how do we harness the lessons of blink without falling prey to its pitfalls? The key lies in 'priming.' Think of your mind as a garden. The seeds you plant (the information you expose yourself to) and how you tend to them (how you process and reflect on that information) decide what grows. You're cultivating a richer, more nuanced decision-making landscape by priming your unconscious with diverse experiences and perspectives. Each new experience is another brushstroke on the canvas of your unconscious mind, making your intuitions richer and more nuanced.

Practice makes perfect, but not any practice. Engage in "deliberate practice." Create scenarios where you must make rapid decisions, then reflect on the outcomes. Was your snap judgment correct? If not, why? Reflective practice helps fine-tune your intuition.

Air traffic controllers are masters of this balanced approach. Every moment counts in air traffic control. Controllers don't have the luxury of lengthy deliberations or second-guessing. They rely on a tuned mix of instant pattern recognition and gut instinct, honed through years of experience.

Controllers intuitively make split-second decisions but know when to slow down and analyze. They've trained their minds to focus on what matters, filtering out the noise. This ability to 'thin-slice,' to make judgments based on thin slices of information, is a skill that transforms your business decision-making and frees you from the trap of paralysis analysis.

As a business leader, your organization needs to develop the ability to find the critical factors in any situation. You don't have to do this alone. It's unreasonable to expect business leaders to master the same skills as air traffic controllers to be effective decision-makers. However, successful leaders can build a team that achieves the same results.

Use diverse perspectives. Surround yourself with a team that brings unique experiences and viewpoints. Their insights help check your biases and enrich your decision-making.

Now, a word of caution: while the air traffic control model offers powerful lessons, it's not a perfect analogy for business leadership. The business world often has more ambiguity and long-term consequences than aviation's immediate, concrete factors. Be mindful not to oversimplify complex business problems or create unnecessary stress by treating every decision as a potential crisis.

Unlike the obvious safety priorities in air traffic control, business decisions often involve nuanced ethical considerations. As you cultivate rapid decision-making skills, don't lose sight of your values and the broader impacts of your choices. Strive to balance short-term pressures with long-term and ethical considerations.

The goal isn't to turn your office into a high-stress control tower. Instead, it's adopting the mental models and decision-making techniques that make air traffic controllers so effective and adapting them to the unique context of your business.

As you sharpen your decision-making skills, picture yourself in that control tower. Feel the weight of responsibility, the thrill of guiding your business through challenges. With the right mindset and practice, you can infuse the precision and confidence of an air traffic controller into your role as a business leader. Your team, your customers, and your business will thank you for it.

A Lesson in Poor Decision Making

My $50 Million Mistake

I confidently eyed the renewal of a contract we had owned for fifteen years. Our documented past performance, a key part of every government selection decision, spoke for itself. Over the following five years, we were 'guaranteed' more than $50 million in revenue. But as I soon learned, assumptions are costly in government contracts.

The government wanted to stimulate competition and move away from sole-source awards. They introduced new guidelines to the contract offices, encouraging the increased use of small businesses. For this contract, a small business classification meant an average annual revenue over the prior three years of under $30 million. The government program office required at least three eligible and interested companies to categorize this contract as a small business set aside.

I made my first mistake here. I assumed that bidding as a small business was in our best interest. It reduced the number of competitors. After all, we were the incumbents, and this was the path of least resistance. We sought advice, which confirmed that we met the criteria. It felt like a slam dunk.

The contract was a small business set aside. Three companies bid, including us, and we won. Or so we thought. That's when the house of cards tumbled.

The competitors filed a protest, and our small business status was under scrutiny. The verdict? They rejected our bid because our growth has pushed us over the $30 million threshold.

Choosing not to register our interest as a small business, we quickly realized, would not have changed the fact that only two competitors were in the bid. Instead of the contract being ours, I watched a $50 million opportunity slip through our fingers.

On reflection, I see the flaws in my decision-making:

Overconfidence: I relied on our incumbent status and past performance. This blinded me to potential risks and alternatives.

Insufficient due diligence: While we sought legal advice, we didn't think of validating the advice. I was showing confirmation bias, i.e., favoring information that confirmed this was a slam dunk.

Assumption-based strategy: I assumed that bidding as a small business was the best way. I didn't explore alternatives.

Lack of scenario planning: I didn't consider the outcome if our small business status was challenged.

Tunnel vision: Focusing on winning the contract as a small business, I overlooked the possibility of a full and open bid.

What were the alternatives? Several things come to mind:

A more thorough analysis of our financials, including projections, may have flagged the risk of exceeding the small business threshold. We knew we were near the limit, but we focused on meeting the threshold and ignored the niggling thoughts that we did not make it.

I should have developed contingency plans instead of fixating on one approach, including preparing for small business and full and open bid scenarios.

Engaging more stakeholders, including financial experts and team members with diverse perspectives, giving valuable insights, and highlighting potential pitfalls.

A formal risk assessment to show the possibility of a protest and our vulnerable position.

This experience taught me a valuable lesson about thorough analysis, diverse perspectives, and flexible planning in decision-making. Relying on past successes or if what worked before will continue to work is not enough.

This $50 million mistake became an expensive teacher. It reshaped how I approach decision-making. Now, I strive to challenge my assumptions, seek diverse opinions, and have a Plan B (and C and D) ready to go.

DESTINATION ONE - RESEARCH AND EVALUATION

Finding Your Starting Position

Let me tell you about Alex, a confident and charismatic product manager promoted to vice president of a tech business after years of increasing responsibility. He had a gut feeling about where the market was heading. "We don't need extensive research," Alex said in the first executive meeting. "I know our customers. I know our market. Let's move fast and disrupt!"

Eighteen months and a large squandered investment later, the "disruptive" new product had fallen flat, and the promising new market had disappeared.

What went wrong? Alex fell into the trap that often ensnares new executives, the myth of the all-knowing leader. Intuition alone is like controlling planes without radar (it happens); you hope your intuition and the systems and processes will be enough. It is possible, but it's more complex.

So, how do you avoid Alex's fate? Embrace research as your superpower. The data and information you collect are the foundation that allows you to peer into the far reaches of your business future. It doesn't show you one future - it illuminates many potential paths, each with its opportunities and pitfalls.

But wait, I hear you cry, "Research is boring! It is dusty reports and mind-numbing spreadsheets!"

Let me stop you right there. The research is anything but dull. It is a reminder of the past. A journey of discovery, an adventure into the unknown territories of your market, becoming a detective, piecing together clues about your customers' deepest desires, competitors' secret strategies, and the hidden trends that reshape your entire industry.

THE REVEAL

Who is Alex?

Let me share a secret with you. That Alex story hits closer to home than you know. You see, once upon a time, I was Alex.

An ambitious product manager (yours truly) had hit the jackpot. My first product, a simulator for training air traffic controllers, had become a success and a record-breaking phenomenon. We're talking about the largest contract in the company's history, scratch that, the largest in the entire industry's history, a record that stands over 20 years later. I was riding high, feeling invincible. A few years after the big win and two promotions later, a chat with a sales rep triggered an idea. Our simulation technology applies to pilot training. The industry was clamoring for a solution to the dead radio in the flight simulator issue. Radio communications were an essential part of pilot workload and cockpit resource management. Until now, synthesized radio communications in flight simulators were poor or non-existent. I, drunk with success and confidence, was too eager to solve that problem.

"The market wants it!" I said, pointing to several industry articles. "It's a natural evolution of our successful product. We'd be fools not to jump on this opportunity!"

Oh, how the folly of success blinds us! In my haste to seize the moment to cement my reputation as the golden boy of product management, I skipped the research.

Did we bother to find out if the market would pay the price point we needed to cover our ambitious development costs? Nope.

Did we take the time to find which specific market segments will be potential customers? Not a chance.

Did we build a solid business case for those theoretical customers?

Why bother? It was a guaranteed success.

Did we predict the hostility from seasoned pilots who didn't like the idea that they needed to be trained to talk with air traffic control? No!

And most critically, did we consider how a regulated industry would receive our product? Cue the crickets.

Fast forward 20 years, yes, two decades, and the sting of that lesson still smarts. The market wanted it, but didn't know what to do with it. We had created a new market but didn't capitalize. The company no longer sells that product.

After many years, we shelved the product as a non-revenue-generating distraction. Other companies found moderate success where we stumbled, but many of the questions we neglected to ask about regulation and about the business case still linger, unanswered.

Now, you might think, "Come on! You had a massive success under your belt. Surely that counts for something?"

And you'd be right, to a point. Past success was a factor in my career progression. I made it from an inexperienced software test engineer to CEO, but success is not a crystal ball. It is downright dangerous if it leads you to assume that lightning will strike twice in the same way.

Here's the reality: The business world isn't a meritocracy where the best product wins. It's a complex ecosystem where timing, market readiness, regulatory landscapes, and other factors play roles. How do you navigate this complexity? You guessed it, thorough, systematic research.

So, what's the takeaway from this cautionary tale? Is it to never trust your instincts? To be paralyzed by the need for perfect information. Absolutely not. That is as dangerous when leading and managing a business as it is in air traffic control. The lesson here is balance and respect for the process.

The beauty of business is that every misstep and failure is a lesson that lights the road ahead. My Alex moment taught me the invaluable importance of rigorous research. It transformed me from a cocky product manager into a wise, still cocky, and battle-scarred business leader.

I pass this wisdom on to you. May it save you from your Alex moment and guide you toward making informed, research-backed decisions in your business journey.

TALES OF THE SEA

Setting Course

I was a ship's navigator on oil tankers an eternity ago.

There was no GPS; our technology was a radar, binoculars, a sextant, and a ship's chronometer. Close to land with recognizable features, assuming the visibility permitted, position fixing was easy. However, the featureless environment of an ocean passage complicated and sometimes made it impossible to fix a position. We relied on the stars. We calculated the approximate latitude and longitude at dawn and dusk, the only times it was possible to see the stars and the horizon together. The window for finding our position lasted only a few minutes. We calculated and plotted a straight line from the star sightings on a celestial navigation chart. With two star sightings, the lines intersected, showing our calculated position. It was as accurate with two lines as throwing a dart at the chart. With experience, there were moments within that small window of opportunity where five or six observations were possible. There was an immense sense of satisfaction seeing the crossing lines showing your position within 10 square miles.

So, how did we find our way across thousands of miles of featureless oceans? How did we know what direction to head if we did not know our starting point? We used dead reckoning (educated guesses). With estimated currents, ship speed, and course, a position within a few square miles was possible.

Not knowing where you are is manageable in deep oceans. Imagine sailing in shallow rocky waters, with only a rough location, and enveloped in thick fog. As land draws closer, the potential for disaster grows.

Internal Research

The State of the Union

Leaders often find themselves so focused on the horizon that they lose sight of the ground beneath their feet. Yet, to chart a meaningful course forward, one must first understand where they stand. This is where internal research comes into play, an often overlooked part of organizational management.

Internal research is not crystal ball gazing or making grand predictions. Instead, it's taking a deep, honest look at the present state of your organization. It's akin to a doctor performing a thorough check-up, not to forecast future illnesses but to understand the patient's health. This involves more than crunching numbers or reviewing financial statements. You must take the pulse of your organization at every level.

Internal research seeks to paint a comprehensive picture of your company's current reality, from the shop floor to the boardroom, from the front-line employees to the c-suite executives. Think of it as creating a high-resolution snapshot of your organization. This snapshot captures the visible aspects like, organizational structure and processes, and the less tangible elements, such as employee morale, relationships, and internal communication dynamics.

The goal is not to judge or criticize but to understand and uncover the unvarnished truth of your organization's strengths, weaknesses, challenges, and opportunities as they now exist. This truth-seeking mission requires a willingness to ask tough questions and, more importantly, to listen to the answers without preconceived notions or defensive reactions.

Internal research is both an art and a science. It combines rigorous data analysis with a nuanced interpretation of human factors. It requires a delicate balance of quantitative metrics and qualitative insights. Done well, it provides leaders with a clear-eyed view of their organization's current state, warts and all.

This understanding serves as the information funnel for strategy exploration and decision-making. After all, how do you plot a course if you don't know your starting point or what obstacles are in your way? Internal research provides that starting point, grounding your plans in the present realities.

ASSESSING THE CURRENT STATE

A Holistic Approach

The financial performance is pleasing; you are cruising and have happy shareholders. Then, from nowhere, that startup erodes your market share and steals your customers. You have no plan to ward off the threat; you didn't need it, you thought, looking back at your past successes. The financial results that follow do not paint a pretty picture.

Knowing where you are is not a colorful chart showing the details of revenue, margins, and EBITDA.

The exercise to understand the organization's current state is about listening, really listening, to what's happening across every level of the company. The research step captures where the organization stands, unfiltered and uncensored.

Understanding the current state is getting a feel for the organization's day-to-day operations, the challenges teams face, and the victories, big or small, that otherwise fly under the radar.

This applies to more than top leadership. Painting a complete picture involves voices from every corner of the organization. The goal is to gather different perspectives, creating a more nuanced understanding of the company's current state. It's fewer ticking boxes and more of an understanding of the organization, providing a context for realistic and inspired strategies. Employees' perspectives, especially those on the front lines, are more valuable than the view from the executive's floor. Listening to your organization will deliver insights that show underlying issues, unexpected strengths, and opportunities that a more rigid analysis overlooks.

I've lost count of the reorganizations I saw in my career. It was like clockwork; the CEO announced another reshuffling whenever the year-end numbers fell short. We'd move a few people around, hand out promotions, and tinker with the org chart. It felt like we were doing something, but we were rearranging deck chairs on the Titanic.

Typically, a small group of executives cooked up these grand plans huddled in a conference room or expensive offsite location, confident they have their fingers on the organization's pulse.

So, what's the alternative? How do we break free from this cycle of ineffective change? Instead of playing "pin the tail on the donkey" with the organization, I went straight to the source: our employees. But, employees clam up when faced with micromanagement and disconnected leadership. They don't share their honest thoughts and feelings.

I began with simple questions.

What's working well?

What's not working?

If you had a magic wand, what would you change?

I know what you're thinking. "Employees won't open up and share their honest thoughts!" And you're right. Trust is earned, not given. So, how do we cultivate where employees feel safe to speak up?

Getting to a state where employees feel safe is a challenging part of organizational management. Honest internal research and continuous improvement begin with 'psychological safety.' Let's explore how to foster such an environment.

Foremost, leadership sets the tone. Leaders must show that they value open communication and diverse perspectives. This goes beyond mere lip service. A leader responding to feedback sends a powerful message throughout the organization. For instance, instead of becoming defensive, a CEO who thanks an employee for pointing out a flaw in a new initiative models the behavior they want to see.

Transparency is another factor. Leaders foster an environment where honesty is valued over perfection by communicating challenges and being willing to admit mistakes. Set up regular "town hall" meetings where executives share successes and setbacks, inviting questions and comments from employees.

Creating formal channels for anonymous feedback is beneficial. Suggestion boxes, anonymous surveys, or third-party reporting systems offer avenues for employees who otherwise hesitate to speak. However, action must be visible, or employees will lose faith.

Training plays a vital role as well. Train managers to give feedback and receive it. Employees benefit from training in constructive communication techniques. This helps ensure that when people speak up, they do so in a way that's more likely to be well-received.

Align recognition and reward systems with the goal of open communication. If employees see their colleagues recognized for bringing issues to light or suggesting improvements, they're more likely to do the same. This is as simple as public acknowledgment in team meetings or as formal as including "contributes to improving processes" in performance review criteria.

It's essential to separate idea generation from idea evaluation. Too often, people reject ideas at the first hint of potential problems. Instead, create forums where ideas are welcomed and recorded before any evaluation occurs. This encourages people to speak up without fear of immediate criticism.

Enforce policies protecting employees who raise concerns in good faith. Employees facing adverse consequences for speaking up undoes years of trust-building.

Patience and persistence are key. Psychological safety doesn't happen overnight. It needs consistent effort and reinforcement. Leaders must emphasize the importance of speaking up and show it through their actions.

THE OFFICE MOVE

The Dilemma of Competing Priorities

In one of my first challenges as the COO, I had to combine two offices into one location. The employees understood the logic behind the decision, cost, and resource optimization, but I had to solve the emotional part of the problem.

The two offices were 40 minutes apart in light traffic, two hours or more during a Montreal snowstorm. Employees lived within reasonable commuting distance of their respective facilities, so upset was the obvious consequence of dropping one location and moving into the remaining building.

The solution was not for management to impose a choice. The senior management team was based in Orlando, so the location had little impact on our lives. We left the choice up to the employees. With general guidelines issued by the C-Suite, a team of employees, with feedback from everyone, found and chose a new office.

It sounds like a recipe for chaos, but it was a success. Not everyone was glad; it is optimistic to expect that. The employees chose a location equidistant from each of the original offices and central to public transport. The outcome showed the force behind mutual trust and autonomy.

We made the findings available to everyone. Employees understood that addressing everything was not practical. They voted on what was most important to them. To promote trust, we set timelines against each initiative. Progress, or lack of it, was visible to everyone.

The trick was channeling friction into forward motion, not a corporate food fight. We want the type of disagreement that sharpens minds, not one that dulls spirits. Think less 'group hug' and more 'productive powder keg.' When employees feel safe to speak their minds, organizations gain access to a wealth of insights and ideas that drive innovation and improve processes.

Knowledge is Power

Research and Situational Awareness

The radar screen paints a vibrant picture of aircraft trajectories, a symphony of movement. Suddenly, a conflict alert blares, shattering the illusion of control. Two converging tracks, minutes from intersecting, demand immediate action. Multiple solutions exist; the controller's instincts scream "Left turn!" for the inbound plane, creating a space between it and the conflicting track. "Turn left heading three one zero," a split-second decision made under pressure.

But the relief is short-lived. Another conflict alert erupts, this time involving a departing plane from a nearby airport, its path now intersecting with the adjusted trajectory of the inbound flight. The air traffic controller realizes the error of the first choice, giving a flurry of instructions to regain safe separation.

Later, as the adrenaline subsides, the sting of near failure lingers. Replaying the scenario, what information could have prevented this close call? Perhaps a more comprehensive understanding of surrounding airspace, including expected departure times and routes, would have informed a different decision. A predictive tool highlighting potential conflicts based on projected flight paths might have empowered the controller to choose a different course of action, avoiding the need for a hasty and flawed maneuver.

This story underscores the need to maintain a situational awareness of the immediate airspace, the broader context, and potential future events. Situational awareness comes only from knowledge. Air traffic management requires more than quick reflexes and technical ability. It demands a holistic understanding of the interconnectedness of the airspace, a commitment to continuous learning, and a relentless pursuit of tools and technologies that enhance decision-making and make sure the safety of every flight under your command. The best decisions are those that are informed and not reactive. The best business strategies share the same characteristics. This is why your research approach must be a conscious choice.

The Energy Source for Strategy Exploration

You have decisions to make about the future of the company. Each decision leads you down a different path. Some lead to glory, others to ruin. How do you navigate this dizzying array of possibilities?

I will put this here right up front. You will fail if you cannot answer the question, what do our customers consider as valuable? None of the market data, CAGR, or competitors matters if you do not answer the question and confirm the responses.

The next question for every for-profit business is, "How will we deliver a profitable revenue stream and long-term growth?" The answer:

1. Offer solutions for your target markets that solve their problems

2. Make sure your solution is more valuable to the customer than the solutions your competition offers

3. Have a business plan showing why the customer will pay more for what you deliver than the cost of creating that value

4. Have a strategy that shows how you will deliver more value to the market than your competition

5. Execute the mission to deliver value profitably

Strategy requires rigorous preparation. Before crafting a strategy, immerse yourself in the details, understanding the market landscape, competitive environment, organization capabilities, and external forces shaping your industry. Jumping in headfirst without this foundational research is like taking control of an ATC facility without knowing the airspace. You will survive a few decisions. Eventually, you will miss something critical. Thorough research is the core of discovering and implementing a strategy.

The problem is that we are awash in data; too much data is as blinding as too little. The 'stuff' that we want gets lost in the noise:

Customer Research

- Who is our current target audience?

- What problems do our target audience need to be solved?

- How are those problems being solved?

- What issues do they have with current solutions?

- What are they paying for the current solutions?

- What issues do our current or potential customers have with our existing solutions?

Competitive Research

- Who are our competitors?

- What solutions do our competitors offer?

- What do they charge for those solutions?

- What are the weaknesses of those solutions?

- What weaknesses do the companies display?

Market Research

- What is the market size?

- How healthy is the market?

- What are the current economic conditions in our target geographies?

This is not exhaustive; it is the prerequisite for starting any strategy exploration exercise.

So, where do you start? If you google strategy frameworks, the choices will overwhelm you. A few of the common frameworks include:

SWOT Analysis: This framework examines the internal and external environment of a company by analyzing its Strengths, Weaknesses, Opportunities, and Threats. It's one of the most widely used tools to understand an organization's strategic position.

Porter's Five Forces: Developed by Michael Porter, this framework helps businesses assess industry attractiveness and competitive pressures by analyzing five forces: competition, potential new entrants, the power of suppliers, the power of customers, and the threat of substitutes

BCG Matrix: This tool helps companies decide where to invest by analyzing their product portfolio in terms of market growth and market share. Products are categorized into Stars, Cash Cows, Question Marks, and Dogs.

This is not the forum to discuss the pros and cons of the many frameworks. But, before you investigate and decide on the frameworks, consider the approach to research you plan to take.

Research is not a one-size-suits-all. Let's look at three examples of research: deep dive, horizon scanning, and a balanced approach. Your research path doesn't influence only your strategy; it rewrites your company's future. The research path isn't an academic debate. As you'll see, each approach takes you into a rabbit hole of possibilities, emerging with a hint of the future as distinct as fingerprints. It's like watching alternate realities unfold in real-time.

Path One: The Deep Dive Dimension

In this reality, you opt for a deep-dive research approach. You dedicate resources to understanding the current market and customers.

Actions:

1. Conduct exhaustive user studies with existing customers

2. Analyze every part of their product's performance

3. Do a detailed competitor analysis

4. Map out customer pain points and create detailed user personas

5. Engage with key industry thought leaders and influencers for insights

6. Develop a feedback loop with top customers for continuous improvement

7. Explore adjacent markets for untapped opportunities or customer segments

8. Benchmark industry best practices and emerging technologies for potential integration

Potential Outcome: You uncover product shortcomings that have frustrated customers. This leads to an overhaul that revitalizes your existing product line, regaining market share and customer loyalty.

Path Two: The Horizon Scanning Dimension

In an alternate reality, you choose a horizon-scanning approach. You cast a wide net, looking beyond its immediate industry for emerging trends and potential disruptions.

Actions:

1. Attend diverse tech conferences outside their immediate field

2. Conduct trend analysis across multiple industries

3. Interview thought leaders from various sectors

4. Set up a dedicated innovation team to explore cross-industry partnerships

5. Watch startups and disruptive technologies in adjacent

fields

6. Create a knowledge-sharing network within the company to discuss new ideas

7. Invest in research on emerging regulatory changes that affect future markets

8. Pilot small-scale projects in promising new sectors to assess the feasibility

Potential Outcome: You find an emerging need for your product or services in an adjacent industry. You pivot, applying your core technology to this new market, opening a blue ocean of opportunity.

Path Three: The Balanced Approach Dimension

In yet another reality, you opt for a balanced research approach, combining elements of deep dive and horizon scanning.

Actions:

1. Conduct a moderate-depth analysis of the current market and customers

2. Do a limited trend analysis in adjacent markets

3. Host collaborative workshops with both current and potential new customers

4. Create customer surveys that capture satisfaction with current products and interest in new ideas

5. Conduct exploration interviews with potential customers in adjacent industries

6. Analyze industry reports and market trends to find commonalities between existing and emerging sectors

7. Hold internal brainstorming sessions with product development and research teams to align findings from both markets

Potential Outcome: You enhance the core product while developing a new offering for an adjoining market. This two-pronged approach allows you to keep the current base while expanding into new territories.

Choosing Your Research Reality: Different Paths, Different Futures

As you contemplate these futures, recognize that selecting the proper research approach hinges on a multitude of factors, including the company's overarching long-term goals and vision, the availability of resources such as time, funding, and personnel, stability, or volatility within the current market, and overall risk tolerance and appetite for change. Each approach offers a unique perspective on the future, illuminating distinct opportunities and challenges.

There are no inherently right or wrong choices; diverse realities exist to explore and evaluate, each with potential outcomes and future implications.

The chosen approach will shape an understanding of the business landscape, highlighting some pathways while obscuring others. The research approach will shape strategy discussions and decisions. It will influence the opportunities you perceive, rank risks, and allocate resources.

For instance, the Deep Dive approach leads to discussions heavily focused on product features and customer retention strategies. The Horizon Scanning approach sparks conversations about radical business model innovations and entering new markets. The Balanced approach causes debates on managing a dual-focus strategy and optimizing the allocation of resources between existing and new initiatives.

Evaluation

Putting Your Data to Work

I've seen countless meetings where participants are drowning in data while thirsting for insights. True magic happens when you transform those raw numbers and feedback into a catalyst for change. Let's examine the myriad ways your newfound insights change your business.

You're sitting in your office, surrounded by reports and spreadsheets, the fruits of your internal research labor. But these aren't just stacks of paper or files on your computer. They're a treasure map, and you're about to uncover the hidden gems.

Your first stop? Strategy. Those insights you've gathered are the compass that will guide your long-term journey.

But wait, there's more! As you dig deeper, you'll find the blueprints for process improvement. Like an efficiency architect, you spot the leaky pipes and creaky floorboards in your operations. It's time to renovate, streamline, and build a lean, mean operational machine.

In business, as in life, you can't do everything. But with your data-driven map, you're no longer shooting in the dark. Divide your time, money, and energy with precision. But a business is only as good as its people. That's where employee development comes in. Your data is a personal trainer for your workforce, identifying where they need to bulk up their skills and where they're flexing their professional muscles.

And let's not forget the customers, the lifeblood of any business. Your research has given you a backstage pass to their thoughts and feelings. Use it to choreograph a customer experience that will have them giving you a standing ovation.

Your data isn't only a bunch of numbers and feedback. It's a Swiss

Army knife of business tools, ready to help you slice through challenges, screw together solutions, and file the rough edges. If you use it wisely, you'll be amazed at the transformation possibilities.

Knowledge isn't only power; it's profit, progress, and potential.

A Structured Approach to Analyzing Information

How do you transform raw data into meaningful insights that drive smart decisions? The key is a systematic approach to analysis. Here's how:

Organize Your Data into Relevant Categories

Start by sorting your data into meaningful groups: financial performance, customer feedback, operational metrics, employee satisfaction, and so on. This organization makes it easier to spot patterns and ensures that comparisons are apples-to-apples. Consistent formatting is crucial here; it streamlines the analysis and reduces errors.

Spot Patterns and Trends

Dive into each category to look for recurring themes or patterns. Are sales increasing over specific periods? Does customer satisfaction dip at certain times of the year? Pay attention to trends over time and correlations between different metrics. For instance, you might find that improvements in employee satisfaction lead to higher customer satisfaction scores.

Benchmark Against Standards

Context is everything. Compare your data against industry benchmarks or your own historical performance. This helps you understand where you stand—are you leading the pack or falling behind? Benchmarking illuminates areas of strength and highlights opportunities for improvement.

Consider External Factors

Your business doesn't operate in a vacuum. Market conditions, seasonal fluctuations, economic trends, and unexpected events can all impact your data. By factoring in these external influences, you'll gain a more accurate and nuanced understanding of your performance.

Challenge Your Assumptions

Data analysis is an opportunity to question preconceived notions about your organization. Be open to surprises, the numbers might reveal strengths you weren't aware of or weaknesses in areas you thought were solid. Let the data challenge your beliefs and guide you toward truth.

Collaborate Across Departments

Two heads are better than one, and a diverse team is even better. Involve team members from different departments in the analysis process. Their varied perspectives can uncover insights you might have missed and help identify blind spots in your interpretation.

Prioritize the Most Impactful Insights

Not all data points are created equal. Focus on the most impactful or urgent issues that emerge from your analysis. Rank these insights based on their potential effect on your business. This prioritization ensures that your efforts are directed where they can make the biggest difference.

Translate Insights into Action

For each key finding, ask yourself: What does this mean for our business? What actions should we take? How will this inform our strategy or operations? Turning insights into concrete action plans is where analysis translates into growth and improvement.

Validate Your Conclusions

Before jumping into action, take steps to confirm your conclusions. This might involve deeper data dives, discussions with stakeholders, or small-scale testing of your ideas. Validation reduces risks and increases confidence in your decisions.

Document and Communicate Your Findings

Finally, document your analysis methods and key findings. Prepare to share these insights with various audiences within your organization, from executives who need the big picture to front-line employees who will implement changes. Clear communication ensures everyone is on the same page and working toward common goals.

By embracing this structured approach, you transform data from a confusing overload into a powerful tool for informed decision-making. The ultimate goal is not just to understand where you are now but to leverage that understanding to shape a more successful future. Data becomes not just numbers on a page but a roadmap guiding you toward your strategic objectives.

THE NOT A STRATEGY MEETING

A Gathering of Gripes

"We need a strategy offsite!" "The sales team is flying in five days. You're leading it," said the CEO. "How about more notice to prepare, boss," I responded, sarcasm obvious for him to detect.

I was the vice president of something. My understanding of strategy was as clear as a foggy runway. But, hey, I was game; I had attended many 'strategic planning' off-sites. I was an air traffic controller in a past life, and of course, I knew how to 'Wing it,' no pun intended.

Five days later, I faced a room full of eager salespeople and senior management, their eyes gleaming with anticipation. I kicked things off, exuding an air of strategic brilliance I didn't have.

What ensued was less of a strategy session and more of a venting marathon. We discussed features the sales team needed, customer complaints about slow deliveries and bugs, and each client's unique wish list. It was a whirlwind of tactical issues.

By the end of the day, my head was spinning. I learned a lot, mainly about our sales team's inner workings and challenges. But as for a strategy? I was still flying blind.

The meeting was a classic example of mistaking a plan for a strategy. We were so focused on the immediate and tactical that we lost sight of the bigger picture and made no meaningful decisions. We hadn't defined our long-term direction or value proposition.

Caught up in the everyday challenges, we neglected to chart a course for the future, relying solely on gut feeling and hoping for the best.

That meeting was a valuable, albeit painful, lesson. It taught me that strategy isn't about firefighting or pleasing everyone. Tough choices, setting a direction, and rallying the team behind a shared vision were necessary. That's a lesson I'll never forget.

The "Not a Strategy Meeting" highlighted a common pitfall for organizations - conflating plans with strategies.

While plans are essential for tactical execution, a strategy concerns vision, direction, and competitive advantage, making choices that set your business apart in the long run.

Before beginning a strategy meeting, consider this: What are the decisions you need to make? What are the overarching goals?

It will save you from another 'Not a Strategy Meeting.'

Managing the Unthinkable

Air Traffic Control on 9/11

The morning of September 11, 2001, began like any other for air traffic controllers across the United States. Routine chatter filled the airwaves as planes took off, cruised, and landed in a well-orchestrated aerial ballet. But, at 8:46 a.m. Eastern Time, everything changed.

As reports of the first plane striking the World Trade Center reached air traffic control centers, confusion reigned.

At the Air Traffic Control Command Center in Herndon, Virginia, Ben Sliney was facing an extraordinary first day on the job as National Operations Manager. As events unfolded and the scale of the attack became clear, Sliney made an unprecedented decision: ground every plane in United States airspace.

The order went out at 9:45 a.m. "All planes are to land at the nearest suitable airport." In the history of American aviation, this was the first time this command had been issued.

Across the nation, controllers sprang into action. Their task was monumental: guiding over 4,000 planes to the ground in hours. This wasn't only a matter of directing planes to the nearest runway. Controllers had to consider fuel levels, airport capacities, and the growing panic among pilots and passengers.

But the challenges didn't end there. Hundreds of planes were approaching the United States from overseas, with nowhere to land. The solution came from an unexpected quarter: Canada.

In an extraordinary act of cooperation, Canada launched 'Operation Yellow Ribbon.' Transport Canada, the Canadian equivalent of the FAA, began preparations to accept hundreds of diverted flights.

Controllers in Canada faced their daunting task. They had to guide planes to airports across the country, from major hubs to small airfields in remote towns. Gander International Airport in Newfoundland, Canada, typically handles 6,000 weekly passengers. That day, they received 38 wide-body planes carrying over 6,600 passengers.

Back in the U.S., controllers worked tirelessly, their voices steady as they guided pilots through the chaos. In control centers, staff taped paper flight progress strips to the walls, creating impromptu information displays as they tracked the progress of each flight.

As the hours passed, the skies gradually emptied. By early afternoon, only military and emergency flights remained airborne.

The events of 9/11 tested air traffic control like never before. Controllers faced an unimaginable scenario with no playbook to follow. Yet they grounded thousands of planes without a single accident through their professionalism, quick thinking, and international cooperation.

In the following days, these same controllers faced the equally daunting task of gradually reopening the skies.

The response of air traffic controllers on 9/11 is a testament to their ability to execute a complex, unprecedented plan under extreme pressure. The system and the people who made it work saved countless lives and became a model for crisis management in the aviation industry.

THE ATC SYSTEM'S RAPID ADAPTATION

Strategy Execution

The Air Traffic Control system's ability to adapt during the 9/11 crisis proved the impact of a well-prepared, flexible organization in unprecedented circumstances.

September 11, 2001, tested America's resolve. It was a brutal, real-time examination of the air traffic control system's strategy and execution capabilities. And, when it mattered most, that strategy proved its worth in spades.

A controller at Newark Airport, hands shaking and mouth dry, exemplified the human element behind the response. His words, "surreal" and "horrifying," underscore the emotional backdrop against which this execution played out. This wasn't a sterile boardroom exercise. This was a strategy in the trenches, with lives on the line.

The ATC's response was impressive, and it was a textbook example of strategic thinking and flawless execution under unimaginable pressure. Here's why it matters to every business leader:

First, let's discuss the value of an overarching strategy. The ATC's primary mission - ensuring air safety - never wavered. When Ben Sliney called to ground every plane in U.S. airspace, he wasn't pulling a Hail Mary. He was executing the ultimate expression of the ATC's core strategy. Safety first, everything else be damned.

This unwavering commitment to their strategic priority separates the wheat from the chaff in business. When the s!*t hits the fan, does your team know what matters most? Do they make tough calls based on your core strategy? If not, you're setting yourself up for failure.

Now, flexibility. The ATC's playbook didn't have a chapter on "What to do when terrorists turn planes into missiles." But their strategy was flexible enough to adapt to the unthinkable. Controllers improvised, creating ad hoc systems to track diverted flights and coordinating with Canada to handle the overflow. This wasn't chaos - it was agility in action.

In business, your strategy can't be a straitjacket. It must give your people the freedom to adapt when the unexpected happens. Because trust me, it will happen.

Let's not overlook partnerships. The coordination between the U.S. and Canadian authorities wasn't a happy accident. It was an alliance that paid off when it mattered most. In business, the right partnerships distinguish between thriving and dying when a crisis strikes.

Remember, strategy isn't only what you plan to do in business. It's what you execute when the world turns upside down. That's the actual test of leadership.

DESTINATION TWO - STRATEGY

No Value Creation Without a Strategy

The movie Pushing Tin portrays air traffic controllers as thrill-seeking, adrenaline-fueled mavericks with cavalier attitudes who juggle the lives of countless passengers. In the film, a picture is painted of a facility where they make split-second decisions with little regard for the structured processes that keep the skies safe. Although entertaining on screen (and a box office failure), the truth is that air traffic control is vastly different.

Strategy isn't a buzzword or a fancy term to throw around in board meetings. It's the beating heart of successful value creation. In business, where change is the only constant and competition is fiercer than an upset Honey Badger, a solid strategy isn't a 'nice to have'; it's your ticket to survival and your passport to thriving.

Strategy isn't a set-it-and-forget-it. It's a living entity that needs constant care and feeding. Your ability to pivot and refine your strategy on the fly is as important as coming up with a brilliant plan. This section is your crash course in dreaming up a killer strategy, bringing it to life, and keeping it fighting fit. By the time we finish, you will have the skills and knowledge to tackle the wild business world and create value that will amaze your competitors.

Far from the chaotic image seen on screen, ATC is a profession where precision, discipline, and strategy are paramount. Controllers work within the National Airspace System (NAS) framework, a complex network designed to make sure safe and efficient movement across the country.

An overarching strategy governs every part of this system. As air traffic control relies on a strategic approach to managing the complexity of the skies, a successful business strategy requires plans, ongoing research, and adapting to changing circumstances.

STRATEGIC OR TACTICAL

What is the Difference?

One of the most common mistakes when creating a strategy is confusing strategic decisions with tactical ones. While both are essential to a business's success, they serve different purposes. Strategic choices focus on the long-term direction and vision of the entire organization, defining its mission and overarching goals. Tactical decisions concern executing those strategies through short-to-medium-term actions, often at the departmental level. It is confusing at first, so to help you, whenever someone offers a strategy, answer the question, is this a measurable initiative, e.g., increase revenues? In which case, it is tactical. It is a step in executing a strategy. Or does it set the direction, e.g., we will pursue mom-and-pop businesses by offering our accounting software tailored for nonprofessional accountants?

Misunderstanding or conflating these two levels leads to ineffective plans, where businesses focus too much on day-to-day operations without aligning them with broader objectives. You spend time in the weeds, the minor details, and dilute the focus on what matters, the strategy. You must learn to separate the two for your strategy exploration to succeed.

	STRATEGIC	**TACTICAL**
FOCUS	Long term and high level decisions that set the direction and vision.	Short to medium term, focused on how to execute the broader strategic plan.
SCOPE	Typically affect entire organisation and its fundamental aspects. Example mission, vision, values and overall goals.	Often departmental or functional, involving specific actions and process.
TIME FRAME	Longer time horizons and may involve planning for several years.	Shorter time frames
EXAMPLES	Entering new markets. Example, Expanding product lines M+A	Budgets: Marketing campaign production schedules optimizing process.

Strategic or Tactical

A Lesson in Poor 'Strategy' Meetings

The Board Comes to Town

Three new members, heavy hitters in the defense and tech sectors, were joining our U.S. board. Their seniority was intimidating. We had a room full of department directors and VPs eager to impress. The meeting aimed to discuss ways to boost our lackluster revenue and allow the Board Directors to meet 'the Dream Team.'

Then it happened. The vice president of engineering presented his plan. This VP had previously and unsuccessfully presented the idea in his budget request. This was his moment to shine before the board members and convince them to back the project.

A customer had paid us a hefty sum to develop an add-on to one of our existing systems. "Let's adapt it and sell it to other customers!" he said, his eyes gleaming.

One of the new board members, a seasoned veteran with a no-nonsense demeanor, asked. "Is this a regulatory need?" "Yes," the VP replied. "And how many potential customers are there?" Questioned the director. "Nearly 200," he answered, neglecting to mention that most were not realistic targets. And how much did we charge our customer?" he asked.

Without missing a beat, the board member declared, "That's a simple decision. That's 30 to 40 million in revenue! Let's do it!"

The room erupted in murmurs of agreement. It felt like we'd struck gold.

"Interesting idea," I said, keeping my voice steady. "But have you completed a preliminary business plan or a return on investment calculation?"

The VP stammered, "Not yet."

I took a deep breath. "Before we allocate a chunk of our R&D budget, why don't you do one? It is premature to decide."

Of course, the retired colonel, unused to being questioned by someone he considered a subordinate, did not receive the contrary opinion well. I dug in my heels.

Four weeks later, the VP returned with a fifty-slide presentation. This time, there were no board members present. After 60 minutes of death by PowerPoint, the last slide was stark: "There isn't a business case for proceeding."

The silence in the room was deafening. The $30 million dream had evaporated.

This incident highlighted everything wrong with our 'strategy meetings.' We'd jumped on a shiny idea without due diligence, blinded by the allure of quick revenue. We did not consider the costs, the market demand, the competitive landscape, or even the basic feasibility of scaling. It was a classic case of emotional decision-making trumping rational analysis.

A strategy meeting is something other than a brainstorming session for half-baked ideas. It provides a forum for rigorous analysis, where participants scrutinize and debate strategic, not tactical, ideas with data. We needed to shift from chasing quick wins to building a sustainable long-term strategy. We needed to ask tough questions, challenge assumptions, and decide based on facts, not wishful thinking. The $30 million mirage taught us an important lesson not to be overlooked. (narrator's voice, "But we did.").

WHAT IS STRATEGY?

A Simple Question – Many Answers

Let me first declare that I dislike the word strategy because companies overuse it, misunderstand it, and apply it badly. You will not get a consensus if you ask one hundred strategists to define strategy. My LinkedIn feed is an endless stream of opinions and advice on strategy. This inconsistency is confusing, especially to those needing the most guidance. However, it will be more confusing to define an alternative word, so let's stick with it.

Here is one example of the definition. Strategy is an organization's overarching plan and direction to achieve its goals and objectives. It involves making choices and trade-offs to position the organization for long-term success in its competitive environment.

The elements of the strategy include:

1. Vision and Objectives

2. Competitive Positioning

3. Resources Allocation

4. Capabilities and Competencies

5. Strategic Initiatives

It's OK as a definition; I argue that points three and five are part of strategy execution, not strategy itself. Point four is part of the research that feeds the strategy creation activities.

So, what is a strategy?

A Strategy Is:

- Informed by data

- A product of vision, desire, passion, ambition, and intuition

- Executed through processes

- Structured by systems and rules

- Made successful by motivated, engaged, energized people and wrapped in a culture guided by supportive and attentive leaders

But what does that mean? Think about strategy as the intended outcomes, i.e.,

1. What problems do you solve? The value you offer for your target audience.

2. Who do you solve them for? The target market/ideal customers.

3. Where do you solve them? What regional restrictions are you imposing (if any)

4. Why do you do this? The vision statement.

5. What solutions to the problems do you offer? i.e., we will solve problem X by offering solution Y. It's your value proposition.

6. Why will your target customers choose your solutions over the competition? Differentiators.

7. What do you want to achieve, and by when? Your aspirations.

8. What grounds you? Your non-negotiable values.

Let's continue our strategy exploration.

The Who, What, and Why of Strategy

Does Order Matter?

In the game of strategy, every move counts. Yet, one of the most impactful decisions a company faces isn't the endgame, but how to make the opening move.

Do we first scout the battlefield, name our target market, and craft our weapons to suit their needs? Or do we forge our best tools first, then search for the battles where they'll prove most effective?

This decision sets the course for a company's future state. Get it right, and you will change the world. Get it wrong, and you find yourself with a brilliant solution to a problem no one has, or worse, forcing a square peg into a round hole of market needs.

Take the target market first approach. Picture yourself digging into the lives and minds of your potential customers. You're collecting data, breathing their experiences, understanding their hopes, fears, and frustrations. This intimate knowledge becomes your compass, guiding every decision from product design to marketing strategy.

The beauty of this approach lies in its laser focus. When you truly understand your customers, you speak their language, anticipate their needs, and create solutions that feel tailor-made. It's like being the friend who knows the perfect gift to give because you've been paying attention. Beware of the blinders this approach creates. When focused on a specific group, you risk missing the overall perspective beyond the fine points. Innovations that could revolutionize multiple industries never see the light of day because they don't fit neatly into your predefined market box.

Now, let's flip the script and consider the problem-solving first approach. Imagine you're an inventor in your workshop, surrounded by your tools and abilities. You're not constrained by what a specific market needs; you're free to dream big and create solutions to problems people do not realize they have. This approach leads to groundbreaking innovations. Think of how many world-changing products started as solutions looking for a problem. The Post-it note, penicillin, and even Viagra were unexpected discoveries that found their markets after the fact.

The risk, of course, is that you pour your heart and soul into creating the perfect mousetrap, only to discover that the world has moved on to digital pest control. Without that market insight to guide you, you're sailing without a chart - exciting but potentially treacherous.

So, does order matter? Yes, but perhaps not in the way you think. The most successful companies don't treat this as an either-or proposition. Instead, they do a complex dance between market insight and innovation.

It's a continuous feedback loop. You start with a general sense of your strengths and the problems you solve. You find potential markets where these solutions resonate. Then, you investigate those markets, learning everything. But you don't stop there. You return those insights to the drawing board, refining and sometimes completely reinventing your solutions. Then, it's back to the market for another round of feedback.

This iterative method allows you to harness the best of both worlds: the innovative spirit of the problem-solver and the customer-centric focus of the market researcher. It's a challenging balance to maintain, but those who master it meet market needs and shape and create new markets.

As you contemplate your strategy, consider your unique circumstances. What's your company's DNA? Are you market visionaries able to read the pulse of consumer needs? Or are you technical wizards capable of solving problems others haven't noticed yet? Your strengths, resources, and the nature of your industry will play a role in finding the right balance.

The order matters less than your ability to keep market and innovation in a constant, dynamic dialogue. Master this, and you'll be well on your way to serving a market and defining it.

Navigating the Skies of Strategy

A Junior Air Traffic Controller's Tale

I was fresh out of training, but at 27, I was older than most first-tour air traffic control officers. When I stepped into the control room, I had the confidence of a fresh graduate and the unwavering belief that every air traffic control problem had a prescribed solution. Little did I know that this control room would teach me more about strategy than any textbook.

As I settled into my training shift with my instructor perched, watching every move, the radar screen was awash with tracks and radar interference. A summer storm was rolling in from the west faster than forecasted. Simultaneously, a Tornado bomber declared an emergency, a hydraulic failure. Its adjustable sweep wings were stuck in the full-back position. With wings swept back, the plane traveled at over 400 knots, over twice its typical approach speed, and as maneuverable as a loaded supertanker.

I realized that my memorized playbook was woefully inadequate. This was not following a preset plan, but executing an evolving real-time strategy and managing multiple interconnected challenges.

As I directed traffic, rerouted planes, and coordinated with neighboring agencies, I was in a cycle of assessment, action, and reassessment. Each decision I made altered the entire skyscape, creating new challenges and opportunities. It was like playing a giant game of three-dimensional chess where the board pieces were perpetually and simultaneously moving.

I soon learned that air traffic control, like strategy, isn't rigidly adhering to a plan or set of processes but maintaining a vision while remaining flexible enough to adapt to changing circumstances.

As the afternoon wore on, I relied less on my training and more on guiding principles. I focused on gathering real-time information. I started running mental simulations, considering each potential action's consequences before committing to an action.

Most importantly, I learned the value of small, reversible decisions. Instead of making sweeping changes, I made incremental adjustments, monitoring their effects and ready to reverse course if needed. This allowed me to navigate the complexity without losing sight of my goal.

By the end of my shift, the skies had cleared, literally and figuratively. We had managed the incoming storm and landed the emergency. But more than that, I gained a new understanding of what it means to execute strategy in a complex, dynamic environment.

I can't help but draw parallels to the business world. How often do companies find themselves in situations where unexpected changes make their plans obsolete? How many businesses falter because they stick rigidly to a plan instead of adapting to reality?

In business, success lies not in perfect prediction or rigid planning but in an evolving strategy in real-time. It's creating a system that senses changes, tests responses, and adapts. The market you sell to is changing. Our job, whether as air traffic controllers or business leaders, is not to predict these changes with perfect accuracy but to build the ability to respond to them. That, I realized, is the true essence of strategy.

Strategy Exploration

Exploration, Not Planning!

I've observed a curious phenomenon in business strategy. I've seen brilliant executives and promising startups fall into the same trap: the allure of strategic planning.

The term itself sounds reassuring, doesn't it? It conjures images of crisp PowerPoint slides, neatly organized Gantt charts, and confident predictions. But traditional strategic planning is often more of a hindrance than a help.

It's time to kill the annual strategic planning meeting. It's antiquated, time-consuming, and expensive. It's time for strategy exploration.

Strategy exploration requires effort, but the payoff comes when you understand and finish your first exploration. Strategy becomes about maintenance. Instead of annual meetings, you adjust and make smaller regular updates.

Let me take you back to a conversation I had with the CEO of a mid-sized tech company. She and her team had recently finished a grueling three-month strategic planning exercise. It included the two-week offsite at an expensive hotel. It concluded with a SWOT analysis, five-year projections, and a meticulously crafted 100-page plan. With pride and exhaustion, she said, "We've mapped out every step for the next five years. We're ready for anything."

Remembering similar convictions early in my career, I smiled. "What if I told you that plan will soon be obsolete?" I said.

Her puzzled look prompted me to explain further. The problem isn't with planning itself. It's with the assumptions underlying traditional strategic planning, assumptions that don't hold up in our volatile, uncertain, complex, and ambiguous world.

Think about it. Strategic planning assumes that predicting the future with reasonable accuracy is possible. It assumes that strategy is a linear, step-by-step process. It separates thinking from doing and planners from executors. In short, it provides an illusion of control in a world that increasingly defies control.

Technological tsunamis don't give a damn about your five-year plan.

Take Artificial Intelligence (AI), for instance. It's changing the game; it's flipping the whole table. A machine learning or natural language processing breakthrough renders a strategy that looked rock-solid last year obsolete overnight.

Do you remember when everyone thought they had e-commerce figured out? Then came AI-powered personalization and predictive analytics, turning the industry on its head. Companies that were busy perfecting their SEO scrambled to integrate AI chatbots and recommendation engines. The rise of AI-generated content is making traditional content mills obsolete. AI-driven logistics are rewriting the rules of supply chain management. And let's not get started on how AI is revolutionizing product development and customer service. In this AI-driven world, your strategy needs to be less of a pre-planned road trip and more of a real-time GPS. You don't want the message "When possible, make a legal U-turn." You want your GPS to say "obstruction ahead" while presenting several rerouting options. Suppose you're still following last year's directions; you're going to miss your destination and find yourself in a completely different business landscape with a map that needs updating.

So, what's the alternative? This is where I introduced strategy exploration. Instead of plotting out every move years in advance, strategy exploration embraces uncertainty. It's a continuous activity of sensing, experimenting, and adapting.

Imagine if, instead of that 100-page plan, your team had developed a set of hypotheses and a series of smaller experiments to evaluate them. Imagine if strategy wasn't something you did once a year in the boardroom but evolved based on customer, employee, and market feedback.

This approach has several advantages. It's more flexible, allowing you to pivot when circumstances change. It's more inclusive, involving broader perspectives in the strategy process. It's focused on learning and adaptation rather than the rigid execution of a predetermined plan.

Of course, strategy exploration isn't without its challenges. It requires a tolerance for ambiguity, a willingness to admit you are mistaken, and the courage to change course based on new information. It feels messier and less specific than traditional strategic planning.

But as I reminded the CEO, this approach is essential for survival and growth in a world where disruption is the norm.

As our conversation ended, I saw the wheels turning in the CEO's mind. She saw strategy not as a document to be produced, but as an evolving part of her organization, something to be nurtured.

As more leaders recognize the limitations of traditional strategic planning, they're embracing the more dynamic, adaptive approach of strategy exploration. It's a shift that will separate the companies thriving in our uncertain future from those left behind.

Strategy is creating an organization capable of flourishing in whatever multiverse emerges. And that is strategy exploration.

STRATEGY IS ABOUT REVENUE

Focus on What Matters

Exploration is traveling through a place to find out about it or look for something in it. At the end of strategy exploration, you will learn where your opportunities lie and what initiatives will most likely lead to success.

This exploration is not wandering aimlessly. Every exploration starts with an aim. Let's make it specific. **Strategy is your plan to increase revenue. Nothing else.** Let me explain why that is not as shocking and naïve as it sounds.

Earlier I described the ways you can add value to the business: Increase revenue, improve margins, manage cash flow and pursue mergers and acquisitions.

While improving gross margins and managing cash flow contribute to our aim, they are tactical activities. They are part of the execution phase.

Mergers and acquisitions are strategic, but they are the execution or the consequence of a strategy. Acquisitions are potential solutions to the objectives, i.e., accelerating growth in existing markets or entering new markets. They can be solutions that improve your ability to execute. Acquisitions are not a strategy. Look at these statements:

Compare

'Let's buy a company and then do [This],'

with

'We need to do [This] to add value. A potential solution is to buy a business.'

If you think like the first example, you are doing it wrong. This is a solution that is looking for a problem. The second is a problem looking for a solution.

The acquisition of, or merger with, your business is the ultimate exchange of value. It is not a strategy, but a goal (hostile takeovers are an exception). An acquisition is the culmination of your efforts at building a successful company. It is a get-out-of-jail-free card if you fail. It's when you cash in on the value you've created or decrease your losses.

But the ability to pursue mergers and acquisitions depends on your company's financial health. And ultimately, your company's ability to pursue mergers and acquisitions depends on generating revenue, which is the foundation for everything else.

A strategy is your path to revenue growth. This is simplistic but underscores a certainty: your business can't survive without revenue and the cash it brings if you get it right. Consider revenue as the company foundation. Without it, you can't invest in innovation, expand into new markets, attract top talent, or keep the lights on.

The Strategy Exploration Map

Eight Steps to Revenue Growth

What I'm about to share isn't something you'll find in textbooks or case studies. This is wisdom from decades on the corporate battlefield. Understand the strategy theory, but let me tell you about the reality.

Like me, you have read many posts advising that you create a simple strategy. While that advice is true, the tough part is discovering and deciding what that strategy is. If that were simple, every company would have a successful strategy, and failure would be a thing of the past.

Strategy exploration is far from linear; It's messy, iterative, and often feels like navigating through fog. But that's where the real magic happens.

1. **Strategy Objectives** – Defining what you want to achieve from the exploration process

2. **Market Evaluation** – Do you stick with the market you know or broaden your opportunities in new markets?

3. **Future Market Shifts** – Identify and understand future threats to your chosen markets

4. **Customer Profiles** – Understanding why your customers buy and equally why they do not

5. **Value Differentiators** – What sets you apart from the competition

6. **Strategy Validation** – Is your strategy grounded in reality?

7. **Strategy Choices** – You have options. How do you choose?

8. **Aligning the Organization** – The role of vision, mission, aspirations, and values

First off, strategy objectives. In the boardroom, the luxury of vague aspirations is not realistic. Your strategy needs a heartbeat, a purpose that resonates with the front lines. I've seen countless strategies fail because they didn't answer one simple question: Why? Your aim isn't numbers on a spreadsheet. It's carving out your place in the market, creating value that makes your competition irrelevant. Don't tell me you want to increase the market share. Tell me how you're going to reshape the industry landscape.

Next, the revenue conundrum, existing or new markets. Do you double down on familiar territory or venture into uncharted waters? This isn't pie charts and market analysis. It's understanding your business's DNA and the market's pulse. I've described how we burned millions chasing shiny new markets when the goldmine was under our noses. Conversely, I've watched industry giants crumble because they were too afraid to explore beyond their comfort zones. Your job is to find that sweet spot where your company's strengths align with market opportunities.

Strategy is the future. Let me let you in on a secret: your crystal ball is always going to be cloudy. But that's no excuse for not peering into the future. We don't have the luxury of certainty. You need to become comfortable with ambiguity. Your strategy must be robust enough to offer direction but flexible enough to adapt as conditions change.

Now, to customer profiles. This is unveiling the hidden obstacles of value creation. Your customers aren't just data points or market segments. They're complex human beings with evolving needs and desires. And they rarely know what they want until you show it to them.

I spent a month working in our client's facility. I experienced the pain of a failed product launch and how it affected the customer's business. The insights we gained led to an understanding of what this and other customers valued. It turns out that reliability and a working product were more valued than meeting a scheduled deadline, or squeezing in new nice-to-have features before delivery; who knew? Get out from behind your desk. Live in your customers' world. Understand their pain points, their aspirations, and their unspoken needs.

In a sea of sameness, why will customers choose you? This is differentiation. It isn't having a catchy slogan or a better feature set. It's changing the value equation for your customers. I've seen companies pour millions into marginal improvements when they needed a complete rethink of their value proposition. Your differentiation strategy needs to be bold, it needs to be meaningful, and, above all, it needs to be defensible.

Your strategy looks impressive on paper, but will it hold up in the real world? Have you validated your strategy? This isn't getting a thumbs-up from the board. You need to stress-test your strategy. War-game it. Break it. Check your ego at the door. Your strategy needs to stand up to the harshest scrutiny.

Choosing a strategy is like navigating a multi-factor, multi-choice maze. This is where leaders earn their stripes. You're not dealing with a simple either/or choice. You're navigating a complex maze of interconnected decisions, each with ripple effects. I've been in rooms where I have made multi-million-dollar decisions. Let me tell you, it's never as clear-cut as case studies suggest. You're balancing short-term pressures with long-term vision, weighing quantitative data against qualitative insights. And sometimes, you trust your gut.

Finally, don't forget to align the organization. Your strategy is worthless if it's a document gathering dust on a shelf. It needs to live and breathe in every corner of your organization. This is more than internal communications or change management. It's creating a shared vision that ignites passion and drives action. Brilliant strategies fail because the organization lacks alignment. From the c-suite to the front lines, everyone needs to understand the strategy, why it matters, and how it contributes to its success.

Strategy isn't only analysis and planning. It's leadership, making tough calls with imperfect information. It's rallying your team around a vision and having the courage to see it through, even when it gets tough.

Refer to Appendix A for a practical example of strategy exploration.

Creating Clarity from Complexity

Features v Differentiation

Don't spend time with the wrong mindset. If you want growth, understand the difference between features and differentiators.

The principles are the same whether you are sticking with the same market or expanding into a new one. Must-haves define markets. To sell into a market, you 'must have' a product or service that solves your customer's problems. The must-haves, as it says in the name, are not optional. However, you have many competitors. How do you differentiate? The temptation is to add features. Before you add features, answer these questions:

1. What added value is there for my target market customers from added features?

2. Are the customers willing to pay more?

3. Is it a must-have or a nice-to-have?

4. What is the benefit to our company?—e.g., increased margins, market expansion, market share increase, product reliability improvement (lower support costs).

That last question is important. There are two strategic benefits of adding features. First, more customers will choose you, but it is a weak argument. Customers don't, or more accurately, shouldn't buy features. They buy solutions to their problems. Assume your idea is for new features Why do this? How does added functionality help customers in your chosen market? Are new customers coming for your existing capabilities, or you have inadvertently expanded your market niche?

Think explicitly about what you are doing. Are you expanding your addressable market, or are you filling gaps in your list of must-haves? This is what I want you to take away. Nice-to-have feature addition is not a way to differentiate without understanding the broader context. Do not confuse a change in market dynamics caused by adding features with increased market share from added differentiation.

How to Compete?

Set Yourself Apart

It's not enough to just "show up" with a product that meets basic customer needs. Businesses that thrive are those that go further, developing solutions that not only solve problems but also stand out in ways that resonate with customers. To do this, companies need to think about strategy in three layers: Entry Essentials, Winning Differentiators and Market Expansion. Let's break down how these layers work and how each one builds toward creating lasting customer loyalty and business success.

Entry Essentials: The Must-Haves

To enter the market, your product must solve the essential problems your target customers face. Think of these essentials as the "price of admission," the baseline solutions that customers expect to see if they're going to take your product seriously. For example, if you're building accounting software for small businesses, your "must-haves" might include basic features like tracking sales, managing expenses, and monitoring cash flow. Without these, you can't compete.

However, must-haves are not one-size-fits-all. Each customer segment has its own unique set of essential needs. For freelancers, this might include simple tax tracking. For small companies, payroll integration could be critical. These needs are non-negotiable; they're the reasons customers will even consider buying your product. But they're only the start.

Winning Differentiators: Standing Out in a Competitive Market

Now we're at the heart of what drives success, differentiation. You've covered the basics and grown your market, but your competition sells the same must-haves to the same people.

Taking a greater revenue share from your chosen market requires differentiation. If you want customers to choose you over the competition, you need to offer something they can't get elsewhere.

Differentiation is not about what customer problems you solve; it's about how you solve them.

Differentiation is delivering solutions in a way that creates unique, high-value experiences for customers. Let's go back to our accounting software example. Say that your customers demand accounting software with built-in bank connectivity functionality. You and your competitors offer the same feature, connectivity, so how does a customer choose? To standout, you enhance the connectivity feature to include robust online security and data protection, giving users the comfort of knowing fraud prevention measures protect them. Or, you focus on price, positioning yourself as the most affordable option. Or you offer 24/7 customer support, giving users peace of mind and added convenience.

Each of these differentiators offers value beyond the basic solution. Your product is more appealing and, more importantly, more valuable in the eyes of your customers. In fact, in this example, customers will pay more for a solution that meets their needs in a way that's faster, easier, or more secure than alternatives.

Market Expansion: Growing Your Addressable Market

Once you've covered the must-haves and differentiators in your existing markets, you can start thinking about expanding your addressable market. This means developing new solutions that address the needs of additional customer segments, allowing you to serve a wider audience. For example, if your accounting software serves freelancers and small businesses, adding features for larger businesses (like inventory management or team collaboration) broadens your market reach.

But here's an important point, expanding your addressable market doesn't mean success. It simply means you now have more potential customers to sell to. Success comes from how you approach these additional needs and from ensuring that each new solution you add truly solves a problem that customers care about. Market size is less important than market success. For instance, is 50% market share of a small market, financially better for your company than 1% of a much larger market? Does the larger market have more established and robust competition?

How to Build Each Layer: A Simple Framework

To put this together, think about your strategy in three layers:

1. Identify the Must-Haves for each customer segment: What essential problems does your product need to solve just to compete?

2. Differentiate with Purpose: By identifying unique ways to deliver added value. Ask yourself: What's the one thing that makes your solution a choice more than your competitors?

3. Expand Your Market Thoughtfully: By identifying adjacent customer needs, you can solve with new features or services. Which segments can you serve without losing focus on your core customer?

Measuring Success at Each Stage

Success looks different at each layer. To stay on track, here are some metrics to consider:

- Entry Essentials: Measure customer satisfaction and retention within your core segment. Are customers sticking around because you've delivered what they need?

- Winning Differentiators: Assess the win rate against competitors and customer loyalty. Are customers choosing you over others, and are they coming back for more?

- Market Expansion: Track growth in new customer segments. Are more customers finding value in your additional solutions?

These metrics not only guide your progress but also help you adjust your approach based on real customer feedback and market trends.

A Relatable Analogy: The Three Layers in Action

Think of your business strategy like running a successful restaurant kitchen:

The Basics (Entry Essentials): Every restaurant must nail the fundamentals - food safety, consistent cooking temperatures, and proper seasoning. These aren't exciting, but they're non-negotiable. If you can't get these right, nothing else matters. Similarly, your product needs to master the basic features that customers expect just to be in the game.

The Signature Touch (Winning Differentiators): This is your chef's special sauce, unique plating style, or that perfect flavor combination that keeps people coming back. Maybe it's your grandmother's secret recipe or a modern twist on a classic dish. These are the memorable elements that make diners choose your restaurant over others nearby. In business, these are your unique features or approaches that make customers specifically seek your solution.

The Menu Evolution (Market Expansion): Once you've mastered your core dishes, you might thoughtfully expand your menu - perhaps adding lunch service to your dinner restaurant, or introducing catering. But you expand carefully, ensuring new offerings maintain your quality and identity. You don't suddenly add sushi to an Italian restaurant's menu just because it's popular. Similarly, business growth should align with your core strengths while serving new customer needs.

Bringing It All Together

In a crowded market, simply having a solution isn't enough. Successful businesses not only meet the essentials, but go above and beyond by expanding thoughtfully and standing out through powerful differentiators. By focusing on each layer: Entry Essentials, Winning Differentiators, and Market Expansion, you create a path to growth that isn't just about playing in the market but about winning in it.

So, the next time you think about your strategy, ask yourself: Are we covering the basics? Are we growing where it makes sense? And, most importantly, are we doing something that makes us the best choice? With this approach, your strategy does more than compete, it truly thrives.

Your product or service must satisfy the must-haves to take part in a market. The must-haves are the same for you and your competition. You are not competitors if you sell luxury sports cars and next door sells budget-friendly minivans. You share similar markets, i.e., vehicle sales, but your customers differ. Your minivan specs do not sway the wealthy professional considering a Ferrari.

The final takeaway is this: when considering existing or new market expansion, you consider the features and services, i.e., the must-haves. To win in any market, think differentiators.

DIFFERENTIATION CONVERSATIONS

Driving Innovation and Growth

Differentiating your organization is another ongoing conversation that must evolve alongside your company and the changing market landscape. Begin by maintaining a relentless focus on customer value creation. Ask yourself, "How do we add value for our customers?" This customer-centric approach safeguards that your efforts stay relevant and impactful instead of chasing novelty for its own sake.

But differentiating your organization doesn't stop there. Expand your perspective to include business and partner value generation. Explore mutual benefits with collaborations, further distinguishing your offerings in the marketplace.

These partnerships open entirely new avenues for growth and innovation. In the ATC market, multi-billion dollar blue chip air traffic management companies had stronger relationships and better access to government-owned national air traffic service providers. These customers preferred to buy simulators as part of a package that included multimillion-dollar operational air traffic management systems. Instead of seeing the bigger companies as competitors, they became partners.

As you consider how to deliver value, challenge your existing revenue models. Reimagine pricing and monetization strategies. Is a subscription-based model or a freemium version workable? These conversations unlock access to previously untapped market segments.

Don't limit your re-imagination efforts to just revenue models. Periodically take a step back and rethink your business model from the ground up. This bold, disruptive mindset can lead to your organization's most transformative innovations, positioning you for long-term success. Long gone are the days when we bought software (technically bought a license). It seems impossible to avoid the shift to annual software license fees and software as a service.

Of course, transformative innovation must be grounded in exceptional product and service design, pushing the boundaries and asking, "What if?" This spirit of creativity leads to features and offerings that separate you from the competition. But don't forget the significance of easy adoption, removing barriers that prevent customers from embracing your offerings. In one notable case, we jumped on the SaaS bandwagon for our airport driver trainer market. Unfortunately, the target market struggled with the concept of SaaS. Their budget process facilitated purchasing outright. The idea of a lease was too far from their reality.

Finally, make it a regular practice to survey the market for unmet needs. This often uncovers underserved segments ripe for your organization's tailored solutions. By staying closely attuned to evolving customer demands, you position your differentiation efforts for the greatest impact.

Let these strategic conversations flow into and build upon one another, creating a holistic view of your industry environment and the myriad growth opportunities. For example, your customer value creation discussions might lead you to develop unique product features. Revenue model innovation conversations may cause a novel pricing strategy that separates you. By focusing on underserved markets, you might develop a brand positioning that resonates deeply with your target audience.

The goal isn't just to be different. It's being different in a way that matters to your customers and is difficult for competitors to replicate. Whether through quality, personalized experiences, exceptional service, or innovative distribution, your differentiation strategy must address evolving customer needs and preferences.

Don't forget to look in your rearview mirror. If your company succeeds, there will inevitably be a copycat. Remember the adage: Someone will kill your cash cow one day, make sure it's you.

Standing out is being noticed and creating lasting value that keeps customers returning and competitors scrambling to catch up.

The Realization

Shifting Mindsets – From Pricing to Value

We struggled to gain traction in a stagnant and inconsistent market. The product was solid, but it often took over eighteen months from solicitation to buying. Many contracts exceeded that timeframe, and sometimes, customers canceled their plans along the way.

The refrain was the same in proposal preparation meetings: "What are our competitors doing?" Or, more commonly, "What price undercuts the competition?" The competition adopted the same approach. It was a race to the middle, as we competed on price. A strategy that was unsustainable in an industry of bespoke systems and custom software. While we won the largest share of contracts, we were losing money.

Competing on price presented us with challenges. The contract specifications were often subjective; vendors submitted a proposal based on their interpretation of the specifications. If the requirement states to include monitors, do you price seventeen-inch monitors or twenty-seven-inches? In price-driven procurement, there was no option but to price at the lowest cost interpretation of the requirements. Proposal submissions from each vendor were not an apple-to-apple comparison.

What price do you choose? Suppose you do not want to rely on luck for the lowest-price lottery draw. In that case, you give the lowest price acceptable to your company, even if that meant low margins. This was not a sustainable business model. Because the customer chose the contract winner based on the price, a few thousand dollars, in a million dollar bid, often lost a contract.

We spent R&D money on adding new features intended to wow customers. When the cheapest price wins, the customer might like the new features, but they will not pay extra for them. In U.S. government procurement, there is no added weight to your proposal scoring for features not asked for in the proposal requirements. The ROI on new feature development was non-existent.

That's when strategy differentiation appeared (although we did not explicitly know it then). We didn't aspire to be different; we needed to be meaningfully different in a way that mattered to our customers and our success.

This led to intense, often uncomfortable discussions. But they were necessary. We were challenging long-held assumptions and pushing beyond the comfort zone of mimicry.

The breakthrough came with an alternative approach to product development; instead of each customer having bespoke software, we changed the architecture, merging over fifteen individual software versions into two or three. It was an expensive and lengthy exercise, with added headaches from customer concerns, but we had no choice.

Moving from bespoke systems to a platform mindset created our differentiators. Each of our chosen differentiators delivered value to the customers and the company.

Differentiator: Product or Service

Sub Category: Innovation

Customer Value: The product had a superior, more desirable feature set and capabilities that reduced the cost of operation for our customers while improving their controller training quality and output.

Company Benefit: More features reduced the spend on software development for each bid, to match competitive proposal requirements.

Sub Category: Quality

Customer Value: The customers saw value in buying robust systems that they trusted and that maximized availability and increased training throughput.

Company Benefit: Increased sign-up for expanded warranty and simulator-support services, upgrade contracts, and enhanced company reputation, boosting sales.

Category: Customer Experience

Sub Categories: Exceptional Service and Convenience

Customer Value: Customers had access to ongoing upgrades, reassuring them they had a future-proof purchase.

Company Benefit: Customer retention. We reduced the likelihood that customers will go to the market for a replacement system.

Differentiator: Pricing

Sub Category: Value Pricing

Customer Value: We created premium upgrade modules. Those on a budget (the systems we sold were hundreds of thousands and sometimes millions of dollars) bought an affordable simulator and upgraded with value-added features later.

Company Benefit: More sales to existing customers. Selling new features developed for one customer to our other customers was now possible.

Why did the competition not copy us? In a word, volume. We boasted twice as many installations as the competing systems combined.

Within a year, we'd carved out more revenue streams, improved customer retention, ballooned our customer base, and improved gross margins. Our sales of upgraded features to existing customers were as much as double the revenue as that from the support contracts the customers were keen to sign.

We weren't only different; we were relevantly different. To date, the simulator has generated over $1/2 billion in sales and service revenues. We had begun the company's most extended period of profitability in its 30-year existence.

FROM AIR TRAFFIC CONTROL TO CORPORATE STRATEGY

Navigating Pressure, Precision, and the Afterglow of Success

The radar screen pulses with tracks and labels, each representing lives suspended in the sky. An air traffic controller leans forward, eyes darting across displays, fingers dancing over controls. The radio crackles incessantly, a cacophony of pilot requests, weather updates, and instructions.

Time compresses. Every decision carries weight; every command must be precise. The controller juggles a three-dimensional puzzle of planes, velocities, and trajectories. A sudden storm blankets the airspace and forces rapid recalculations. An unscheduled emergency landing throws carefully orchestrated patterns into disarray. Yet the controller's voice remains steady, a calm center in the storm of data and metal.

As the rush subsides, adrenaline gives way to a bone-deep exhaustion. Muscles ache from sustained tension. The controller's mind races, replaying moments and second-guessing split-second choices. Relief mingles with lingering stress, the knowledge that thousands landed safely, tempered by the ever-present awareness of what could have gone wrong.

In the muted aftermath, the air traffic controller takes a deep breath. The weight of responsibility settles like a familiar coat. Pride in a job well done wrestles with knowing that tomorrow will bring fresh challenges. For now, there's solace in routine, logging out of systems, debriefing colleagues, and finally stepping out into a world that is blissfully unaware of the invisible choreography inside.

The intensity of crafting and executing a successful business strategy is comparable to the high-stakes environment of air traffic control. As financial results confirm the strategy's success, executives experience a rush.

Leaders pore over market data, competitor actions, and economic indicators in the c-suite and boardroom. The strategy takes shape, each decision carrying the weight of potential success or failure. The execution phase feels like that busy control tower, a flurry of activity, constant adjustments, and the pressure to make the right call at every turn.

When quarterly reports confirm the strategy's effectiveness, there's euphoria at first. Executives are relieved and triumphant, like an air traffic controller seeing the last flight safely land. The months of planning, sleepless nights, and tough decisions have been worthwhile.

Yet, just as the controller's mind continues to race after a busy shift, business leaders analyze every aspect of their success. Which moves were pivotal? How could they have further optimized their moves? The weight of maintaining this success settles in tempering celebration, knowing that markets, like skies, never stay clear for long.

After the earnings call, leaders take stock. There's pride in seeing the strategy translate to tangible results, market share gained, profits increased, and goals exceeded. But, like air traffic controllers preparing for the next shift, they're already thinking ahead. What's the next challenge? How do we sustain and build upon this success?

The parallels run deep, the intense focus, the high stakes, the blend of exhilaration and exhaustion that follows success. In both realms, there's little time to rest on laurels. The business world perpetually changes, demanding constant vigilance and readiness for the next enormous challenge.

EXPLORATION STEP 1 - STRATEGY OBJECTIVES

Why Are We Doing This?

Strategy! Discussed endlessly, executed poorly, and often misunderstood. Before diving into strategy exploration, let's discuss the fundamental question: What do you want to achieve from the process?

Strategy exploration is setting the stage for transformative decision-making. When you begin this journey, you must be clear about your goals. Are you looking to redefine your business by uncovering new market opportunities? Or perhaps you find the Achilles' heel in your current business model before your competitors?

You want to align your organization with a unified vision to drive growth for the next decade. Your objectives will shape every following step and dictate which parts of strategy exploration deserve the lion's share of your attention. If you're gunning for market expansion, you'll need to double down on customer profiling and future market shifts. If it's refining your value proposition, you'll want to pour your energy into differentiation strategies. Don't dive into strategy exploration without an end game, only to emerge with a jumble of data and no actionable insights. Don't fall into that trap.

Define your objectives and use them as a compass to navigate the complexity of the process. Do you want a roadmap to enter a new market? A plan to outmaneuver an emerging competitor? A blueprint for overhauling your value proposition? Be specific. Be bold. And most importantly, make sure these objectives tie directly to your overarching business goals.

The clarity of your objectives at this stage will decide the power and relevance of your ultimate strategy and how you divide your resources throughout the exploration. Get this right, and you've laid the foundation for a strategy that drives actual business results.

You might not know what you want. That's okay. It's not unusual for inexperienced strategists to get stuck here. Work through the steps in order. They elicit new ideas and confirm them. If you are unsatisfied, return and revisit the sections that need improvement.

Why are the exploration steps are in the order they are? There is an argument for rearranging some of them. But, at the end of the process, you will have a list of potential and prioritized initiatives (differentiators). The choice of initiatives requires informed decision-making. For example, how do you ask for ideas for differentiators without first understanding your markets, customer problems, or potential market shifts? Each step informs one or more future steps. The order adds focus and boundaries. Don't waste time discussing ideas for new markets if new markets are not practical.

Exploration Step 2 - Existing or New Markets

The Revenue Conundrum

If revenue is the strategy's focus, one question looms: How do we grow it? Do we stick with our existing markets or move on to new markets? Or do we delicately balance the two? These are your considerations. Simple when you break it down.

One of these paths leads deeper into familiar territory, your existing market. It's a path you know well, with its challenges and opportunities. The other path stretches into uncharted territory, new markets full of potential and pitfalls. Which do you choose?

You are a chef working in a bustling restaurant and considering opening a food truck in an unknown part of town. That's the essence of the difference between existing and new markets in strategy.

Existing Market

It's your bustling restaurant. You know the customers, their tastes, and your competitors. Your strategy here is maintaining or expanding your share of the market.

Key characteristics:

1. Established customer base

2. Known competitors

3. Clear market boundaries

4. Understood customer needs

5. Existing distribution channels

Strategic focus:

- Customer retention
- Market share growth
- Product line extensions

Challenges:

- Intense competition
- Price pressure
- Market saturation
- Customer loyalty to established brands

New Market

Now you're launching that food truck. It's exciting, but you're in uncharted territory. Your strategy here is creating and defining the market itself.

Key characteristics:

1. Undefined or emerging customer base
2. Unknown competitors
3. Unclear market boundaries
4. Unmet or unarticulated customer needs
5. Lack of established distribution channels

Strategic focus:

- Market education
- Creating demand
- Establishing brand awareness
- Rapid iteration and learning

- Building infrastructure and ecosystems

Challenges:

- High uncertainty

- Need for customer education

- Potentially longer path to profitability

- Difficulty in forecasting demand

The big difference? You're fighting for a bigger piece of a known pie in an existing market. In a new market, you're baking a whole new pie and convincing people they're hungry and want your new pie.

Take Apple. They weren't entering the existing mobile phone market when they launched the iPhone. Apple created a new market for smartphones. They had to educate consumers, build an ecosystem (remember "There's an app for that"?), and essentially change how people thought about their phones.

On the flip side, when Apple launches a new iPhone model, it competes in an existing market. They focus on incremental improvements, maintaining market share, and fending off competitors.

The approaches for each are vastly different. You might focus on operational excellence, cost leadership, or product differentiation in existing markets. In new markets, it's innovation, flexibility, and creating value in ways customers might not realize they need.

Remember, though, the lines can blur. Sometimes, entering a new market disrupts and redefines an existing one. Ask Blockbuster about Redbox and Netflix, or ask Blackberry about Apple.

The key takeaway? Know which market you're dealing with. It will shape your strategy, resource allocation, and success metrics. Choose wisely!

EXPLORING EXISTING MARKETS

The Safe Option

It's often safer and more profitable to focus on what you do best in markets you know well. And there's wisdom in this approach. After all, you've got a foothold, understand the terrain, and overcome the challenges peculiar to this market.

The strategy for growing revenues in existing markets is not marketing campaigns, redesigned websites, social media, new sales hires, or adopting advanced CRM tools. These are parts of execution.

Many companies confuse growing their existing market by simply selling more of their current products to more customers. While increasing your customer base is important, true market growth involves finding additional problems to solve or creating more value for your current customers. Let me share a powerful example that illustrates this difference.

Consider a company providing medical imaging software to radiology departments in mid-sized hospitals. Their core product helps radiologists view, analyze, and store medical images efficiently. A traditional growth approach might focus on selling this software to more hospitals or convincing existing customers to buy more licenses.

However, real market growth comes from understanding your customers' broader challenges and leveraging your existing capabilities to solve them. Here, they realized that their deep understanding of radiology workflows and imaging technology positioned them to solve additional problems their customers faced.

Think about it this way: If you're already in the radiology department helping them manage images, what other adjacent problems do you see? What additional value could you create with your existing knowledge and capabilities?

The medical imaging company identified several opportunities:

1. Radiologists struggled with preliminary diagnosis efficiency

2. Departments needed better ways to collaborate with specialists

3. Quality assurance and compliance reporting consumed valuable time

4. Resource optimization was a constant challenge

5. Patient outcome tracking was manual and time-consuming

These weren't new customers or markets, these were the same radiology departments they already served. The difference? They were solving fresh problems and creating additional value by extending their core capabilities.

This approach transforms the company from a simple image management vendor into a comprehensive radiology workflow and analysis platform. They didn't need to find new customers; they created more value for their existing ones by solving more of their problems.

This is true market growth because:

1. It leverages your existing relationships and credibility

2. It builds on your core competencies

3. It creates additional revenue streams from existing customers

4. It strengthens your competitive position

5. It increases switching costs as customers adopt more solutions

The key insight here is that growing your existing market isn't doing more of the same; It's solving more problems or creating more value for the same customers. You're already there, you understand their challenges, and you have their trust. Use that position to identify and solve adjacent problems or enhance your current solutions to deliver more value.

Consider your own business: What additional problems could you solve for your current customers? How could you create more value with your existing capabilities? The answers to these questions often reveal significant growth opportunities hiding in plain sight within your existing market.

It's easier and more profitable to solve additional problems for existing customers than to find new customers for existing solutions. Your current market likely holds more growth potential than you realize. You just need to look at it through the lens of problems to solve rather than products to sell.

This approach to market growth provides a clearer path to value creation, stronger customer relationships, and sustainable competitive advantages. It's not about selling more; it's about solving more.

Don't make a hasty decision. Develop a nuanced understanding of your current position and potential. Think strategically, considering every angle, weighing opportunities against risks, and preparing for multiple scenarios.

Sometimes, the answer is not an existing or new market proposition. A hybrid approach, strengthening your position in existing markets while cautiously exploring new ones, is the best path forward.

As you ponder these questions and analyze the data, remember it's the beginning of the process. Suppose the signs point towards exploring new markets. In that case, you'll need to embark on a new analysis, identifying which markets to consider, assessing entry barriers, understanding new customer segments, and more.

But for now, focus on mastering your current domain. Dive deep into the data, challenge your assumptions, and paint a vivid picture of your market position. Only then will you have the information to decide whether to entrench or expand.

A Tale of Two Simulators

New Market Ideas are Easy, Execution?

We had a dominant market share in an inconsistent, price-driven market, air traffic control tower simulators. Magnificent systems where large wraparound screens displayed detailed 360-degree 3D out-of-the-window tower views of the airport, complete with planes and vehicle movement further enhanced with weather and sound effects.

Our services business revenues were growing, but we needed something else to offset inconsistent and lower-margin simulator sales.

We repurposed the existing technology and intellectual property to offer a product to train people to drive around an airport. The idea made sense; we had the expensive components, the 3D airport scenes, and the plane and vehicle movement simulation.

The value proposition; reduce the millions of dollars in yearly damage caused by careless and unaware airport drivers colliding with planes and to reduce the number of unauthorized vehicles entering active runways.

Investment in the new product was minimal. The market potential was attractive.

There was excitement and interest in the product, but it was a commercial failure. We sold a few. The sales brought in revenue, but the product became a distraction. The revenue gains did not justify the marketing effort or further investment.

Why? The product did not offer perceived value to the target customers. There was no regulatory need or insurance company directives to create demand. The customers were new to us; they used an unfamiliar budgeting and purchasing process and had little to gain commercially from this added expense.

We did not complete a new market assessment; new technology was insufficient for an appealing value proposition. It was another cool idea, but a solution seeking a problem.

IDENTIFYING NEW MARKETS

Considerations Before Entering New Markets

When your existing market no longer meets your corporate financial objectives, it's time to consider the monumental task of entering new territories. But this isn't the moment for hesitation or cautious tiptoeing. We're not inching forward; we're charging headlong into uncharted territory, seeking the key to your company's next successful leap. Your core competencies aren't just skills on paper; they're battle-tested strengths ready to be deployed in fresh arenas. Now is the time to cut through the noise and uncover genuine opportunities that can redefine your company's trajectory.

Harnessing Your Strengths

Begin with what you do best. Your core competencies form the bedrock of any successful expansion. Deploy them where they'll have the most significant impact. Pay attention to your existing customers; their evolving needs often point toward untapped potential and new avenues for growth.

Anticipating Industry Shifts

Industry trends are the early signals of change. Spot them before others do, adapt swiftly, and position yourself ahead of the curve. Don't let geographical boundaries confine you. Seek markets where your capabilities can truly shine, transcending borders and unlocking new possibilities.

Exploring the Value Chain

Examine the value chain—opportunities often lurk both upstream and downstream. Leverage strategic partnerships, fill gaps in the market, and strengthen your overall position within the industry. By understanding every link in the chain, you can identify where to exert influence and gain a competitive edge.

Assessing the Competition

Approach potential new-market competition with clear-eyed objectivity. Identify their weaknesses and the gaps where your unique value proposition can give you a distinct advantage. This isn't about underestimating the competition; it's about understanding them thoroughly to position yourself effectively.

Reading Economic Indicators

Economic signs matter. Vigorous growth, increasing consumer spending, and favorable demographics are all signposts pointing toward promising markets. However, be wary of opportunities that seem too easy. Often, the most rewarding ventures require overcoming significant barriers, which can also serve as protective moats once you're established.

Focusing on Growth Potential

While market size is important, it's the growth potentialthat should ignite your interest. Look for rising sectors where your companycan establish a forceful presence early on. Remember the power of synergy—theideal market doesn't just accommodate your existing strengths; it amplifiesthem.

From Shortlist to Strategy

As your shortlist of potential markets takes shape, eachoption represents a different future for your company. Now the actual workbegins. Analyze each possibility thoroughly. Strategize boldly. Your company'sgrowth trajectory hinges on these crucial decisions.

Taking Decisive Action

Which new market aligns best with your overarching goals? Where can you make the most significant impact? The moment for decisive action has arrived. Make informed choices, move with purpose, and watch as your company's influence expands into new territories.

Evaluating markets is exciting and fraught with risk. Even the largest companies set themselves up for failure. Air France's launch of Joon, a millennial-focused airline, is an excellent example.

Introduced in 2017, Air France positioned Joon as a trendy and lifestyle-oriented airline, with branding positioning it more as a fashion brand or rooftop bar than a traditional airline. The idea was to appeal to younger, digitally savvy travelers by incorporating organic smoothies and hipster aesthetics. However, this strategy confused consumers, employees, and investors alike, as the branding did not communicate the airline's purpose or value.

Despite initial growth and plans to expand the fleet, Joon struggled to achieve profitability. By 2019, Air France admitted that Joon's brand identity was perplexing and folded the airline into its principal business.

Target expanded into Canada, opening over 100 stores rapidly, to capitalize on brand recognition among Canadian consumers familiar with Target's U.S. stores. But, the company faced supply chain issues, leading to poorly stocked shelves and higher prices than in its U.S. stores. Target misjudged the Canadian retail landscape, facing strong competition from established local players. By 2015, Target exited Canada, losing around $5 billion.

In the early 2000s, eBay attempted to capture the Chinese e-commerce market by acquiring EachNet, a local online marketplace. The company didn't adapt to China's unique market dynamics, such as integrating local payment systems and understanding consumer preferences. Meanwhile, local competitor Alibaba's Taobao offered free listings and better aligned with Chinese consumers' needs. Market share dwindled, and eBay closed its China site in 2006.

Home Depot, the largest home improvement retailer in the U.S., entered China in 2006 to tap into the country's booming real estate market. The company overlooked cultural differences. Chinese consumers were less inclined to undertake DIY projects than U.S. customers. After struggling to gain traction, Home Depot closed its last seven stores in China in 2012.

As we've seen, even well-known brands run aground when they underestimate local competition, misjudge consumer preferences, or cannot navigate regulatory complexities. The allure of growth shouldn't overshadow the importance of doing your homework. Dive deep into market research, understand the nuances of local cultures, and customize their strategies instead of assuming a one-size-fits-all approach. Testing the waters with pilot programs is a smart move before going all-in. A measured approach is often the key to keeping out of trouble and finding a profitable path forward with new market expansion.

The lesson here, be wary of the weaknesses of human nature. We overestimate our strengths and opportunities and underestimate the competition. The business world is strewn with new market strategy failures. Learn from them and don't make the same mistakes.

Before expending resources on the detailed analysis of new markets, find which ones are worth it. This first screening helps focus your efforts on the most promising opportunities.

What do you do with a shortlist of potential new markets?

A Strategy Breakthrough

How Data Drove Success

My first year as a COO was a whirlwind. In the ten years since I joined the company as a product manager, eight of them were unprofitable. Worryingly, our overhead costs ballooned to nearly 50% of total revenue. This was untenable. Something had to change.

We took care of the cost issue, cutting overheads in the first year to 35% and, over the following eight years, to less than 20%, but that was not enough. We needed revenue growth, and that meant a new strategy.

An analysis of our existing markets showed that selling air traffic management systems and simulators was not viable for sustained growth. We had a nearly eighty percent worldwide market share in ATC simulation. The operational air traffic management segment, another business unit, was highly bespoke, with infrequent and lengthy procurement cycles. The addressable market was not large enough.

Our adopted strategy was to grow our existing market by offering value-added technology upgrades and to add a services business for long-term warranty and on-site systems maintenance personnel. While that proved successful, it had a major shortcoming; it only applied to our existing customer base. Growth depended on winning new systems sales, and they were few.

The secret was in the data. Our largest customer was the United States Government across several federal agencies. The U.S. Department of Defense (DoD) spent approximately $560 million on virtual training (simulation) operations and maintenance, far greater than the system purchasing costs. The addressable market for operations and maintenance, was 50 times greater than our existing market.

Of course, expecting the Lion's share of the new market would be naïve; large companies such as Lockheed Martin and Raytheon were dominant. However, those companies often had a legal obligation to outsource portions of their contracts to smaller businesses; Partnering with them was an option.

Leveraging our extensive U.S. government contract experience and stellar track record, we identified thrilling opportunities in expanding into the virtual training operations and maintenance market. To capitalize on this potential, we established a new subsidiary specifically focused on securing a share of this sector.

But why form a new subsidiary? The government services arena is notoriously cutthroat, with bid rates that must be grounded in reality. To prevent large companies from winning contracts by underbidding at a loss, firms are required to undergo audits certifying that their proposed rates are legitimate. In this environment, where the lowest price wins, creating a new subsidiary afforded us a fresh cost structure with lower General and Administrative (G&A) overheads. This strategic move provided us with a pricing edge over competitors, positioning us favorably in the fierce competition for government contracts.

The new market strategy kicked off the longest continuous profit period in the company's history. It remained profitable until my exit as CEO eight years later. The recurring revenue nature of the business stabilized cash flow and cash generation. Market cap, which had languished in the $20 million to $30 million range, hit more than $250 million.

Our journey from financial instability to sustained profitability illustrates the dynamics of market analysis and bold decision-making. We transformed our company's trajectory by recognizing the limitations of our existing markets and identifying untapped potential in adjacent sectors.

This evolution is a testament to the importance of continual market assessment, willingness to change course when necessary, and the transformative power of a well-executed new market strategy.

New Markets Strategy

Market Assessment

After evaluating the potential for growth within existing markets, you have determined the viability and attractiveness of entering new markets is appealing. This decision requires assessing several factors to ensure that expansion aligns with the company's goals, capabilities, and resources.

However, at this stage, it's not a detailed analysis. Suppose that in the later final stage of strategy exploration, it shows that a new market entry has potential. In that case, a full validation will be necessary.

Entering a new market is a leap that redefines your company's trajectory, yet it demands more than ambition. Success hinges on thoroughly assessing the opportunity's size, growth trajectory, and potential return on investment. This is where you lay the groundwork, envisioning your company's place in an unfamiliar landscape and evaluating the feasibility of your goals. But understanding the opportunity itself is only the beginning.

As you map out the competition, consider who the established players are and what barriers they pose. Knowing the terrain you intend to navigate is the difference between a smooth entry and a grueling uphill struggle. Similarly, the demands and preferences of potential customers must shape your strategy; what works in your current market might not resonate here. Bridging the gap between your existing offerings and local expectations often involves subtle adjustments or a complete overhaul of your approach.

The regulatory environment poses yet another layer of complexity. Every market comes with its own set of rules, compliance standards, and potential pitfalls. Navigating this maze requires foresight and often local expertise to avoid regulatory missteps that stall your momentum. Economic factors further complicate the picture; exchange rates, inflation, and tax implications influence profitability. It's a balancing act of macroeconomic forces that either strengthen or undermine your business case.

Culture plays a role in shaping market entry strategies. Misunderstanding local customs or failing to adapt your messaging goes beyond translation; it's connecting with your new audience. These nuances create subtle but powerful obstacles that impact the reception of brand perception.

In 1997, Walmart, the American retail giant, entered Germany by acquiring two local retail chains totaling 95 stores. With high hopes of replicating its U.S. success in Europe's largest economy, Walmart aimed to revolutionize the German retail sector with its low-price strategy and customer service practices.

Walmart's failure in Germany stemmed from significant cultural missteps: the company introduced American-style customer service practices such as overly friendly greeters and bagging services that German shoppers found intrusive and insincere; it implemented employee policies like mandatory morale chants and restrictions on workplace relationships, clashing with German norms around professionalism and personal privacy; Walmart underestimated local shopping habits by maintaining large, impersonal store formats, and stocking unfamiliar American products, neglecting Germans' preference for smaller stores and local brands; it also underestimated strong local competitors who had deep market understanding and loyal customer bases; Walmart's anti-union stance conflicted with Germany's powerful labor unions, leading to employee dissatisfaction and legal challenges, all of which culminated in a failed venture

After nearly a decade of losses amounting to around $1 billion, Walmart exited the German market in 2006, selling all its stores to a rival.

Alongside cultural considerations, looking at resource requirements is necessary to decide whether you have the financial muscle, human capital, and technological infrastructure for this expansion without overextending your organization.

New ventures complement existing operations, creating synergies that amplify overall success. However, don't overlook the risk of cannibalizing your market share. Your entry strategy, whether through direct export, joint ventures, or acquisitions, sets the tone for the entire effort, shaping challenges and opportunities ahead.

Risk assessment is indispensable, weighing potential pitfalls against expected rewards. This isn't about becoming paralyzed by possibilities but preparing for them. Mitigation strategies for identified risks need to be robust and adaptable. Beyond immediate gains, align your long-term vision; the new market must fit financially, enhance your brand, and sustain future growth.

Financial projections bring these elements into focus. Estimating revenues, profits, and payback periods and comparing the return on investment to other available opportunities makes a compelling, data-backed case for the expansion. Ultimately, new market entry is a commitment of resources and a foray into unfamiliar risks. But when executed with rigorous preparation and a clear-eyed approach, it becomes a powerful driver of growth, diversifying revenue streams and opening doors to exciting new possibilities.

While the promise of new markets is exhilarating, there's a peril in getting swept up in your hype. Passion for your company's potential is important, but blind optimism is dangerous. Don't mistake enthusiasm for evidence. Without a rigorous reality check, bold plans unravel, exposing you to risks you didn't see coming. Temper the allure of expansion with a commitment to validate every assumption; the market doesn't care about your aspirations, only whether you deliver on them.

Exploration Step 3—Future Market Shifts

Strategy is the Future; the Present is Your Launchpad

Ignoring the future is fraught with danger. Many companies no longer exist because the present blinded them. Blockbuster in-store video rental became obsolete in part because of new competition from Redbox DVD kiosks and Netflix DVDs by mail. Netflix made its own DVD by mail obsolete with video streaming.

There are many prominent examples of projects that failed because of market shifts, for example:

The Concorde (1969–2003)

The Concorde was a joint venture between the British and French governments to build and fly a commercial supersonic jet.

Although technologically successful, the rise of cheaper, more fuel-efficient planes and shifts in environmental concerns overtook the project. Noise pollution, high operating costs, and the 1970s oil crisis made the Concorde economically unviable in the long run. The global aviation market moved toward lower-cost, mass air travel, reducing demand for luxury supersonic flights.

California High-Speed Rail (2008–Present)

The California High-Speed Rail aimed to connect major cities in California with fast, efficient rail service.

Political shifts, legal challenges, and rising costs led to the failure. Environmental concerns, changing federal support, and public skepticism over its viability have led to endless delays and down scaling of the original plan. The rise of electric cars and innovations in private transportation further called into question the need for high-speed rail.

Let's look at an example of how future changes impact current decisions.

An airport is considering adapting its infrastructure for the Airbus A380, the largest passenger plane in the world. Operating the larger aircraft will generate more revenue from landing and service fees. However, the runway needs to be lengthened and widened. The parking spots need to be larger, and new passenger bridges are required to make this possible (all tactical initiatives). Before they invest millions in the project, they undertake an exercise in understanding future market shifts.

Sounds exciting, right? But before pouring concrete and moving earth, we must do serious crystal ball gazing.

We're diving into economic forecasts, demographic shifts, and airline strategies. We're considering how technology makes our shiny new runway obsolete before the paint dries (vertical landing vehicles). In this game, the future starts now.

We can't only look at passenger trends. What about cargo? Special events? And let's not forget those "unknown unknowns" that habitually sneak up on us.

So, how do we prepare for this uncertain future? We map trends, plan scenarios, and closely watch emerging tech. We spy on our competitors (legally, of course), anticipate regulatory changes, and scrutinize our supply chains.

And here's a pro tip: Assign timelines and probabilities to these potential impacts. Is it likely? Possible? Or a wild idea that keeps you up at night?

Bottom line: Your future impact analysis isn't a one-and-done deal. It's an ongoing process that keeps your strategy sharp and ready for whatever curveballs the future throws.

So, don't look at where the ball is next time you're crafting a strategy. Look at where it will be. That's how you stay ahead.

The goal is to be prepared for various possibilities. Consistently revisit and update the analysis as new information becomes available.

Your strategy must be flexible enough to adapt to these potential future impacts. Build in trigger points - specific indicators that, when reached, signal the need to pivot or adjust your strategy. This approach allows you to stay agile in the face of changing circumstances.

As the examples of Blockbuster and Netflix show, industries transform rapidly and the rate of change is increasing rapidly. Your future impact analysis must be ongoing, not a onetime exercise. By continuously scanning the horizon and adjusting your strategy, you position your company to thrive amidst change instead of being blindsided by it.

While it's impossible to predict the future with certainty, a robust future impact analysis offers the foresight needed to make informed decisions. By considering potential changes and their timelines, you build a strategy that's reactive to the present and shaped for the future.

Exploration Step 4 - Customer Profiles

Unveiling the Hidden Obstacles of Value Creation

It was early evening in Sydney, Australia. After a long day of investor meetings, I was walking back to the hotel together with Brian, my business sidekick for over two decades, and the sales and marketing vice president. Brian and I worked well together. We shared many achievements and the occasional disaster. Sharp-witted and intelligent, Brian had a stern look that some people found intimidating. We had a similar sense of humor and the same core values, which kept things balanced.

Suddenly, the skies opened up and caught in a downpour, we ducked into a small convenience store. Brian bought two umbrellas that were $10 each. Stepping back into the rain, we unfurled our umbrellas and continued our walk. After a few minutes, Brian said, "I wonder why these umbrellas were so cheap?" On cue, a gust of wind whipped past, and his umbrella flipped inside out, snapping a few ribs and folding it in on itself. "Oh, I see," Brian said without missing a beat.

What is the moral of this story? The convenience store owner understood his customers, people passing by who needed a quick fix. He wasn't worried about repeat business because most of his sales were to those caught unprepared, like us. For a passerby caught in the rain, a $10 umbrella was a small price for immediate relief, even if it only lasted one storm. His customers knew they were buying a quick, disposable solution, and that was enough.

The umbrella supplier understood his market just as well. He catered to convenience stores and similar businesses, offering low-cost, low-quality umbrellas perfect for impulse buys. These umbrellas didn't need to last; they needed to be cheap enough to sell quickly. It was a simple, effective business model built on understanding what his direct customers (store owners) and their customers (people like us) expected. In the end, everyone got what they paid for. Similarly, chefs understand they don't get a Michelin Star by cooking delicious food. Their actual mission is to create unforgettable experiences that keep diners returning for more.

Strategy, often shrouded in complexity, is about one thing: delivering customer value. This explicit understanding transforms a good business into a great one.

If delivering value is the secret to your business, it's also the secret to your customer's business. Value isn't what you think you're offering; it's what your customers gain.

Let me take you through my days designing and selling air traffic control simulators. We thought we were in the business of providing simulation technology that our customers used to train air traffic controllers. Sounds reasonable, right? Wrong. We were in multiple businesses, each serving a different master.

To our government customers, the value of our offerings was simple. To them, our simulator wasn't only a training tool. Air traffic control training is notorious for high washout rates and a shortage of qualified controllers. The simulator was a throughput machine, squeezing more developmental controllers (basic training complete and ready for operational training) from the same raw recruits. But any vendor of ATC simulators offers this.

In their eyes, increasing the number of recruits passing the initial training phase is valuable. Our value proposition was to give them the tools to produce more developmental controllers faster, better prepared for operational training, and cheaper.

Now, shift your gaze to the aviation university deans, their eyes gleaming as they imagined impressed parents and star-struck prospective students. Our high-tech simulators? They were marketing gold, drawing in the brightest minds, and filling lecture halls. The university's value proposition to the parents was that their child gets the best education with the best tools and equipment. An impressive simulator with high-resolution 3D visual scenes of the airport and the taxiing, departing, and landing planes showed this.

Realizing that our customers had different ways of assigning value, our value proposition to the University became that our training simulators had desirable feature differentiators, e.g., speech recognition, sound effects, special visual effects such as weather, fires, explosions, and more. The training capabilities had become secondary in deciding what simulator they chose.

The beauty of this approach lies in recognizing that, while the product remains constant, its appeal morphs based on the specific needs of each customer profile. This approach builds long-lasting relationships by aligning our offering with each unique customer's values.

By refining our message, features, and engagement to address these distinct values, we not only made a sale but also deepened trust and relevance. This nuanced strategy allowed us to serve each sector as though our product was made specifically for them, reinforcing our position in the market and fostering customer loyalty.

So, how do you uncover these hidden value propositions? It starts with curiosity. Dive deep into your customers' worlds. What keeps them up at night? What makes their hearts race with excitement? These aren't idle questions; they're the keys to unlocking explosive growth.

Understand that not every potential customer is the right customer. Strategy isn't saying yes. Know when to say no.

The Customer Value Table

It's Not What You Sell; It's What Value You Offer

You know what markets are workable. This chapter discusses the problems customers in those markets want to have solved.

This is not about what solutions you deliver to solve these problems, but how your solutions solve those problems. Think back to our accounting software. You and your competition deliver solutions that record sales, expenses, and profit. Do your target customers value a solution that reduces the time needed to become proficient? In that case, ease of use adds value. Are the customers cost-driven? This makes price a differentiator.

Imagine you're the CEO of a young tech company. You've developed a promising AI-powered platform for managing complex data, and the first market response has been positive. You've even secured a few key clients. But as your company grows, you must differentiate yourself from the competition to succeed in a crowded market.

Step 1: Understand the Problem

First, you must understand what problems your target customers face and how those problems translate into unmet needs.

Their target customers are mid-sized businesses struggling to manage and leverage large amounts of data. They have several pain points:

1. Data Overload - Businesses have bought a solution to the data storage problem. Overwhelmed by data from multiple sources, they find it difficult to sift through the noise and gain actionable insights.

2. Integration Challenges - Integrating diverse data sources

and systems is complex and time-consuming, hindering the effective use of data.

3. Lack of Expertise - Businesses lack the expertise needed to adopt and manage advanced data analysis tools, leading to inefficient use of their data assets.

Step 2: Identify Competitor Weaknesses

With a picture of your customer's needs, you find where your competitors are falling short. This is the key to your unique selling proposition.

Look for:

Limited Functionality - Are your competitors' platforms lacking specific features or functionalities that are valuable to your customers?

Integration Complexity - Are their solutions challenging to integrate with existing systems or technologies?

Limited Scalability - Can your competitors' platforms handle growing data volumes or evolving business needs?

Lack of Customization - Are your competitors' solutions inflexible and unable to be tailored to specific customer requirements?

Customer Experience - Do your competitors offer exceptional customer service?

Data Privacy Concerns - Do your competitors offer robust data privacy and security features?

Customer Psychology

Need is Not Enough

As important as understanding what customers value and why they buy is the reverse, the hidden reasons they won't buy.

We bought a technology we repurposed with our speech recognition and 3D graphics to offer a virtual reality product to train law enforcement in incident de-escalation.

The media was awash with stories of police and civilian encounters that resulted in physical harm and, many times, loss of life. The adoption of body-worn cameras in many police forces and the increasing use of smartphones with high-resolution video and social media sharing had made the topic front page news.

Our product would help law enforcement agencies train their officers in the art and techniques of de-escalation. There was little wrong with our solutions. We had invested in making it a slam-dunk product that could reduce the violence and killings we were seeing reported in the media, but it didn't sell. Why?

Any department that bought one sent the message that they had a problem with excessive violence. Still, more worryingly, the Police Chief is telling the officers that they are at fault with their heavy-handed tactics.

The problem they attempted to solve instead was not in de-escalation techniques but in handling an escalation. They chose handgun simulators.

Yes, perhaps by identifying what your customers value, you have eliminated what they don't. These are not mutually exclusive. Let me introduce the value equation.

THE. VALUE EQUATION

One Plus One Does Not Equal Two

The value equation says your value proposition must exceed the customer's objections (spoken or unspoken) to your offering.

To understand this, let's draw an analogy from physics: the principle of inertia. In the physical world, setting a stationary object in motion takes more effort than keeping a moving object moving. This same principle applies to business decisions.

The higher the resistance to your offering, the more effort (or value) is required to overcome it. Selling upgrades to a happy customer is easier than acquiring new customers. The first buy from the customer has added inertia to your upgrade offerings.

In the earlier example of the de-escalation trainer, our value proposition was that the customer improves officer training. That is not a value proposition; it's a feature. What are the potential values as perceived by the customer?

De-escalation training improves relations with the local community.

The training reduces lawsuits, and the cost associated with compensation and legal fees.

The first is intangible. How do you assign a value to improved relations? The second value is misstated. The city bears the cost burden in the United States, not the officers or the department.

The resistance to the de-escalation trainer was the customer's unwillingness to accept that the department had a problem that needed to be solved. Sadly, our value proposition did not overcome the customer's objections on the other side of the equation.

Given the peculiarities of government budgets in the U.S., the police chief gives up the money if it goes unused. An alternative buy was the handgun trainer. The value proposition is that weapons skill saves officers' lives. It's obvious why the Chief made that choice. The value proposition is greater than the nonexistent (in the buyer's mind) negative side of the equation.

The takeaway is that the first push to overcome resistance needs to be substantially more potent than the resistance itself. In business terms, the perceived value must outweigh the perceived negatives.

1. **Find the Resistance:** Understand the specific concerns and obstacles that create resistance.

2. **Quantify the Value:** Articulate and, where possible, quantify the benefits of the proposed change.

3. **Address Concerns Directly:** Develop solutions that specifically target each point of resistance.

4. **Overwhelm with Value:** Make sure the total value proposition far outweighs the perceived negatives.

Once you overcome the resistance, maintaining the new state becomes easier, like keeping a moving object in motion.

Do your solutions generate enough 'force' to overcome the natural resistance to change?

One last point. Suppose your competitor has strong solutions to known customer problems. Think carefully about entering the market. Reflect on the value equation and customer resistance to change. Do you add enough new value to overcome the natural resistance to changing what works well? If you cannot, your growth is now restricted to customers new to the market. Your addressable market is smaller. Is this enough, or does the commercial viability need a share of customers that use the competitor's solutions?

Exploration Step 5 - Differentiation

Why Will They Choose Us?

You understand what you do, and who you do it for. You know the approach you will take to grow revenue, i.e., new markets, existing markets, or both. That was the what; this is the how. Knowing what markets you will attack and the customer profiles within those target markets has led to a list of customer problems that you must solve. The solutions are opportunities to differentiate. What does that mean?

Differentiation is solving your customer's problems in a way they perceive to be more valuable to them than competing offerings.

Why does your company purchase goods and services from your vendors?

Hiring consultants is not to help you complete a task. You hire them to create something that has value for you and potentially your customers.

Adopting Generative AI is not to help write marketing copy. You adopt it because it creates marketing copy that returns customer leads or is cheaper than using people, reducing costs and improving margins.

They are not buying the new software interface because it looks better than the competing products. They are buying it because it solves problems in a manner they consider has value:

1. Reduces the time needed to train staff

2. Increases their efficiency and output

3. Cuts their operating costs, increasing margins and profit

4. Leads to more customers

When you think about differentiators, consider why you buy from your vendors; your customers are doing the same (although they might not know it).

Key Concept: What Are Mutual Benefits?

As you consider your strategy differentiators, understand the concept of mutual benefits.

1. What value do you provide to the customer?

2. What value does your proposed solution provide to your business?

For example, do you offer a bespoke delivery to a limited customer base, with a predicted 40% margin, that distracts and delays delivery of products or services to thousands of customers at a 30% margin?

If you cannot correlate a differentiator with a company benefit, look elsewhere for ways to differentiate. Strategic benefits come in many forms, e.g., future revenues, intellectual property that opens new products and markets, or developing new abilities that reduce operating costs. Make sure you find yours. Chasing revenue alone is not a path to sustainable growth.

Value Correlation

Differentiation Examples

Whether innovation, convenience, or emotional connection, a well-crafted strategy emphasizing specific differentiators creates strong customer loyalty and elevates a brand beyond its competition. As you explore this section, your aim is to discover differentiators that complete this sentence, "We are the only company that [Insert Your Unique Value Proposition]."

While the thought of finding one or more differentiators may overwhelm you, the limited differentiation categories described here will help you narrow down how you complete the sentence.

This list describes every class of differentiator, no matter how original.

Group 1: Product or Service

Innovation, Quality, Customization, and Sustainability

Innovation: Customers seeking cutting-edge solutions value innovation as it ensures they get the most advanced products or services.

Example: A technology company introducing AI-driven features for workflow automation. The customer perceives value in being early adopters of timesaving innovations that give them a competitive advantage.

Quality: High-quality products attract customers who value durability, performance, and reliability.

Example: A luxury car manufacturer offering superior craftsmanship and engineering, appealing to customers who want a premium, reliable vehicle.

Customization: Customers who value uniqueness or specific requirements will seek customization to get what they need.

Example: A furniture company that offers custom-made pieces allows customers to design items that fit their style and space perfectly, which enhances personal satisfaction.

Sustainability: Eco-conscious consumers want sustainability because it aligns with their values and desires to reduce environmental impact.

Example: A clothing brand using sustainable materials and ethical production processes resonates with environmentally aware customers who want to decrease their carbon footprint.

Group 2: Enhancing Customer Experience

Exceptional Service, Convenience, Community Building, and Transparency

Exceptional Service: This appeals to customers who want support and guidance throughout their buying journey. It builds trust and loyalty.

Example: A high-end electronics store providing personalized consultations and 24/7 customer support ensures a smooth experience for customers, enhancing their overall satisfaction.

Convenience: Modern consumers value timesaving and hassle-free experiences.

Example: A grocery delivery service with an intuitive mobile app offers convenience by allowing customers to shop from home and schedule deliveries at their convenience.

Community Building: Customers who value shared experiences or social connections appreciate brands that create a sense of belonging.

Example: A fitness company offering group workout sessions and an online community platform, creating camaraderie and fostering a sense of support among its customers.

Transparency: Customers increasingly want transparent information on products, pricing, and business practices, especially those who are value-conscious or skeptical.

Example: A beauty products brand is upfront about its ingredient sourcing and production processes, helping customers confidently purchase safe and ethical products.

Group 3: Branding and Positioning:

Unique Value Proposition, Storytelling, Authenticity, and Emotional Connection

Unique Value Proposition: Customers want to know why they should choose your product over competitors. A distinct value proposition clarifies this.

Example: A software company offering a user-friendly, AI-powered interface for non-tech-savvy users positions itself as the go-to choice for simplicity and ease of use.

Storytelling: Customers are more likely to connect with a brand that shares relatable stories, making the brand memorable.

Example: A shoe brand sharing stories about how local artisans craft its products from ethical sources taps into customer emotions, fostering brand loyalty.

Authenticity: Customers, especially millennials and Gen Z, value brands that stay true to their values and mission without being overly promotional.

Example: A coffee company known for its authentic relationships with farmers and ethical sourcing appeals to customers who value integrity and want to help businesses that align with their principles.

Emotional Connection: Customers who are emotionally invested in a brand are more loyal and often act as brand advocates.

Example: A baby product company creating ads that show actual families' emotional experiences builds a deep connection with parents who relate to the emotional narratives around parenting.

Group 4: Distribution and Access

Selective Channels, Omnichannel Experiences, Direct-to-Consumer Models, and Accessibility

Selective Channels: Customers value exclusivity and curated shopping experiences.

Example: A luxury watch brand sold only through select high-end boutiques creates an aura of exclusivity, appealing to customers who want unique, prestigious items.

Omnichannel Experiences: Customers expect seamless interactions across physical, digital, and mobile platforms.

Example: A retailer offering a unified experience where customers browse online, buy in-store, and return through a mobile app increases convenience, satisfying tech-savvy customers.

Direct-to-Consumer Models: Customers appreciate the cost savings and personalization often offered by D2C models.

Example: A mattress company offering high-quality products only online at lower prices, with home delivery and generous return policies, appeals to budget-conscious shoppers.

Accessibility: Making products accessible appeals to a broader customer base, including those with disabilities or remote customers.

Example: A streaming service that offers content in multiple languages with subtitles and accessibility features reaches a wide, diverse audience, ensuring inclusivity.

Group 5: Pricing Strategies

Premium Pricing, Value Pricing, Freemium Models, and Subscription-Based Offerings

Premium Pricing: Customers who associate price with quality will opt for premium products if they perceive added value.

Example: A luxury skincare brand pricing its products higher because of rare ingredients appeals to affluent customers who equate higher prices with superior results.

Value Pricing: Customers who seek affordability without sacrificing quality will appreciate value pricing.

Example: A discount supermarket offering essential products at low prices targets cost-conscious consumers who want savings.

Freemium Models: This appeals to customers who want to experience a service before committing to buy.

Example: A SaaS company offering a basic version of its software for free, with paid premium features, attracts small businesses that scale up as they grow.

Subscription-Based Offerings: Customers who enjoy convenience and regular access to products and value subscription models.

Example: A meal kit service that delivers weekly pre-planned meals taps into busy professionals who want to save time on grocery shopping and meal prep.

Each differentiator group offers a value that matches customer needs and drives customer satisfaction and loyalty through targeted offerings.

Finally, this list of differentiation categories is common knowledge. If it works for you, it will work for the competition. Focus on differentiators that are defendable.

EXPLORATION STEP 6 - STRATEGY VALIDATION

Is it Viable?

To make a strategy workable, it must have more than a radical idea or an enthusiastic executive team. Before committing resources to a new initiative, assess the underlying assumptions and execution feasibility to confirm or drop the choice. Strategy validation helps organizations avoid costly missteps.

Strategy validation involves three steps:

Success Analysis

The first step in confirming a strategy is defining the essential conditions for success and any roadblocks that prevent them from currently being true. This analysis examines the fundamental assumptions, external factors, and internal capabilities, i.e., the roadblocks that, if not overcome, will hinder the possibility of achieving the desired outcomes.

For example, suppose an organization is considering an investment in a new digital platform to expand the addressable market. In that case, the analysis might show:

1. The projected return must justify the financial investment

2. Customers must be willing to adopt the new digital channels

3. Your organization must have the technical ability to build and support the platform

4. The necessary IT infrastructure and data management capabilities must be in place

Assessing the Reality

The next step is a reality check, which involves taking an honest, objective look at each success factor. Understand what needs to be done to remove any roadblocks.

Let's continue with the digital platform example; the assessment shows:

1. Major Roadblock: The organization lacks the in-house talent to develop and manage the platform

2. Partial Roadblock: The existing IT infrastructure does not meet the platform's requirements

Figuring out Cost and Risk

The last step in strategy validation is to evaluate the cost and risk of eliminating the previously identified major and partial 'roadblocks.' This is not a detailed estimate, but a gut feel approach. Think back to the chapter on Malcolm Gladwell and his book Blink. Pay attention to the experts; their insights come from experience. This analysis helps the organization understand the level of effort, investment, and potential pitfalls in executing the initiative.

The cost and risk assessment for the digital platform example shows:

1. Upgrading the existing IT infrastructure to meet the platform's needs: low cost and minimal risk

2. Hiring and training a team of digital platform specialists: medium-cost and medium-risk

3. Overhauling the organization's legacy data management systems to support the new platform: high-cost and elevated risk

Validation serves as a reality check, ensuring that even the most innovative ideas are grounded in a thorough understanding of the organization's capabilities and the market landscape.

Exploration Step 7 - Choosing a Strategy

The Multi-Factor, Multi-Choice Maze

Strategic decision-making is the moment where analysis turns into action. It's when you stand at the crossroads, armed with data and insights, ready to chart your course. This is when the myriad of possibilities you've uncovered during research converge into a chosen path forward. This stage influences everything from resource allocation to market positioning, shaping your company's future.

However, you are now at the center of a vast decision matrix. Surrounding you are many factors, each being a component that influences your choice. These are financial considerations, market trends, technological advancements, regulatory environments, and potential disruptions. Within each, there are more choices with implications and ripple effects.

It's more than a simple A or B choice. You're facing a complex web of interconnected decisions. Each decision alters the landscape of choices.

> *See Appendix A for a practical approach to resolving the complexity of choosing a strategy.*

Let's examine a few examples:

Differentiator Selection:

In this example, you face a choice. You must choose between offering a high-value solution with lower profit margins and a lower-value solution with higher margins.

Market Expansion:

Do you choose to expand within existing markets with non-recurring revenue, or do you enter new markets with new customers, potentially offering lower margins but promising long-term, recurring revenue?

Within these factors lie multiple choices, and the decision in one invariably affects the others. Choosing an enterprise target market pushes you towards a premium pricing strategy and proprietary technology. Conversely, opting for a consumer market favors a competitive pricing model and an open-source platform.

The Dynamic Maze of Interconnected Choices

The complexity continues. This maze is dynamic. Market conditions shift, technologies evolve, and competitor or customer actions suddenly alter the playing field. A decision that is best today might be obsolete tomorrow.

These are interconnected factors, creating a ripple effect of consequences. Refining one sub-optimizes another, leading to trade-offs. For instance, pushing for an aggressive launch timeline compromises product quality or limits your manufacturing options.

You're dealing with varying uncertainty across these factors, grounding some in data and trends. In contrast, others rely more on educated guesses and gut feelings. Balancing these varying levels of certainty adds another layer of complexity.

But remember, complement these tools with experience, industry insight, and, sometimes, a leap of faith.

Mastering the Maze

The key to mastering this complexity isn't finding a perfect solution, which rarely exists, but making a well-informed, thoughtful decision that aligns with your organization's broader strategy and values. This requires:

- Clearly define your decision criteria and their relative importance

- Gathering comprehensive data on each factor and choice

- Analyzing the interdependencies between several factors

- Considering both short-term impacts and long-term consequences

- Engaging diverse perspectives to challenge assumptions and find blind spots

- Maintaining flexibility to adjust your decision as added information emerges

Navigating a multi-factor, multi-choice decision is less finding the correct answer and more finding a way through a complex maze of possibilities. It requires a blend of analytical rigor, foresight, and the courage to make tough calls in moments of uncertainty.

The leaders who excel in this environment see a broader view and the specifics, understanding the nuances of each factor while keeping a clear view of the overall goal. They recognize that in a world of complexity, the goal is not perfection but making the best possible decision with the information at hand while staying agile enough to adapt as the landscape inevitably shifts.

Exploration Step 8—Aligning the Organization

Vision, Mission, Aspirations, and Values

Imagine trying to build a skyscraper without laying a solid foundation. No matter how impressive the design or how skilled the builders, the structure would inevitably collapse. The same principle applies to businesses. Vision, mission, aspirations, and values are not just corporate jargon; they are the bedrock upon which successful strategy execution is built. They give a business purpose and direction, setting the stage for strategies that are not only practical and data-informed but also inspiring and true to the organization's core identity.

The Guiding Star: Vision and Mission

Your organization's vision and mission answer the fundamental questions: *Why do we exist? What are we aiming to achieve?* This clarity acts as a guiding star for all strategic decisions, ensuring that every step taken aligns with the organization's overarching goals. When everyone understands the destination and the purpose of the journey, aligning efforts becomes natural, and progress becomes intentional.

The Heart and Soul: Aspirations and Values

While vision and mission set the direction, aspirations and values speak to the very heart of the organization. They go beyond business objectives, tapping into the emotional core of what the organization stands for and strives to become. This emotional resonance doesn't just inform policies, it inspires and motivates employees, stakeholders, and customers. It creates a shared sense of purpose that transcends daily operations, fostering deep commitment and unity.

With these foundational elements in place, your organization gains a robust framework for decision-making. Every potential strategy, initiative, or opportunity is evaluated against this framework, acting as a filter to ensure alignment with your core purpose and principles. This clarity not only simplifies complex decisions but also helps prioritize efforts that genuinely matter for the organization's future. It ensures resources are invested where they can make the most significant impact.

Vision, mission, aspirations, and values encourage a long-term outlook. They lift the organization's gaze beyond immediate challenges or short-term wins, prompting consideration of lasting impact and legacy. In a market where short-term gains sometimes tempt businesses away from sustainable practices, this forward-thinking approach is essential. It helps safeguard the organization's future by balancing present needs with tomorrow's possibilities.

Creating these foundational statements isn't a task for the top executives alone. Gathering input from different levels of the organization is crucial. This inclusive approach fosters unity and builds consensus, ensuring that the vision and values resonate with everyone involved. When employees contribute to defining the organization's purpose and values, they develop a collective ownership that becomes a powerful force in driving the strategy forward.

Guiding Focused Research and Analysis

Once established, these elements provide invaluable context for subsequent research efforts. They help focus data gathering and analysis on areas most relevant to the organization's core purpose and aspirations. This targeted approach ensures you don't get lost in a sea of data but instead collect insights that are meaningful and directionally sound. Research becomes not just an exercise in information collection but a strategic tool aligned with your mission.

One of the most compelling aspects of this approach is how it balances ambition and realism. While rooted in the organization's current capabilities, the vision and aspirations stretch it beyond the present. They encourage dreaming big while remaining grounded. This balance results in the development of a strategy that is both inspirational and achievable, pushing the organization to new heights without overextending its reach.

Before you can apply improvements, you need to know where the problems are. Starting at the end—examining your vision, mission, aspirations, and values—allows you to identify misalignments and gaps. It's like diagnosing the health of the organization at its core. This approach ensures that any strategies or changes you implement are not just superficial fixes but address the underlying issues that could hinder success.

By investing time and effort into defining and embracing your vision, mission, aspirations, and values, you lay a sturdy foundation for everything else your organization does. These elements transform from mere statements on a wall into living principles that guide actions, decisions, and strategies. They become the heartbeat of your organization, driving not just what you do but how and why you do it.

In a world of constant change and competition, ensures that no matter the challenges ahead, your organization remains steadfast, purpose-driven, and aligned with its core identity, ready to execute strategies that lead to lasting success.

Let's understand each in more detail.

The Vision: A Company's Guiding Light

A vision shows where the company aims to be in the future. It's aspirational and inspirational.

Consider this vision statement from Tesla: "To create the most compelling car company of the 21st century by driving the world's transition to electric vehicles."

This vision works because it's ambitious and forward-thinking and communicates Tesla's goal. Revolutionizing an entire industry and, by extension, impacting the world.

Contrast this with a poorly crafted vision: "To be the world leader in [Insert Your Industry Here]." Or this classic "Enhance shareholder value and exceed customer expectations."

This vision falls flat because it's vague, generic, and applies to any company. It doesn't inspire or give direction.

The Mission: The Purpose of the Journey

The mission defines the company's existence and what it does for its customers and society.

Take Patagonia's mission statement: "We're in business to save our home planet."

This mission is powerful because it's concise, bold, and clearly states the company's purpose. It goes beyond selling outdoor gear; it positions the company as an active participant in environmental conservation.

Consider this problematic mission statement: "To offer high-quality products and services to our customers."

While not incorrect, this mission is too generic. It doesn't differentiate the company or offer any unique sense of purpose. Many companies deliver quality products or services, so this mission cannot inspire or guide.

Aspirations: The Company's Goals

Aspirations, or goals, are the specific, measurable objectives that mark progress toward the vision. They're like stops on a map, helping a company chart its course and measure its progress.

A well-crafted aspiration is: "To reduce our carbon emissions by 50% within the next five years."

This goal is specific, measurable, time-bound, and aligns with a vision of environmental responsibility. It provides an obvious target for the organization.

In comparison, a poorly defined aspiration is: "To grow the business."

While growth is positive, this aspiration lacks specificity. How much growth? In what timeframe? In what areas? Planning or knowing when the goal has been met is difficult without these details.

Values: The Non-Negotiable Principles

Values are the principles that define a company's characteristics and shape its ethos. They're non-negotiable standards that guide behavior and decision-making at every level of the organization. Values communicate expected behaviors from employees and set standards for customer interactions.

Let's look at examples of well-defined values that translate into specific, non-negotiable behaviors.

Integrity: "We are honest and transparent in our dealings."

Employee behavior: Always give accurate information to colleagues and customers, even when uncomfortable.

Respect: "We treat everyone with dignity and value diverse perspectives."

Employee behavior: Actively listen to and consider every viewpoint in meetings, regardless of the speaker's position.

Customer behavior expectation: Customers treat our relationship with honesty and mutual respect.

Accountability: "We take ownership of our actions and their outcomes."

Employee behavior: Admit mistakes promptly, focusing on solutions instead of blame.

Innovation: "We seek better ways to solve problems."

Employee behavior: Propose and test new ideas, viewing failures as learning opportunities.

Safety: "We prioritize the well-being of our employees, customers, and communities."

Employee behavior: Immediately report or address any safety concerns, never cutting corners that compromise safety.

These values work because they're specific, actionable, and leave little room for interpretation. They clearly define what's expected of employees and what customers can expect from the company.

Contrast these with vague or poorly defined values:

"Quality" - While positive, this value is too broad. Quality in what way? How is it measured?

"Customer-focused" - Again, it's positive but vague. How do employees show this focus?

"Teamwork" - While important, without specific behaviors attached, this means different things to different people.

Values become potent tools for shaping behavior when clearly defined and consistently enforced. They help employees decide aligned with the company's principles and give customers an understanding of what to expect in their interactions with the company.

For example, if "Integrity" is a core value, an employee who increases sales by exaggerating product capabilities knows that such behavior is unacceptable. The non-negotiable nature of the value makes the right course of action straightforward.

Customers who value transparency are drawn to companies that are committed to honest communication.

For values to be impactful, they must be more than words on a wall. Leadership must consistently model them, integrate them into every aspect of the business, and uphold them even when challenging or costly.

When a company truly lives its values, it creates a robust and unified climate that guides behavior, drives decision-making, and ultimately contributes to the achievement of the company's vision and mission. It turns abstract principles into concrete actions, shaping the day-to-day reality of how the company operates and interacts with the world.

THE POWER OF STRATEGY DISCOVERY

Numbers Matter

Do you remember these paragraphs?

Imagine if, instead of that 100-page plan, your team had developed a set of hypotheses about the future and a series of small experiments to evaluate them. Imagine if strategy wasn't something you did once a year in the boardroom but evolved based on customer, employee, and market feedback.

This approach has several advantages. It's more flexible, allowing you to pivot when circumstances change. It's more inclusive, involving broader perspectives. It's focused on learning and adaptation and not the rigid execution of a predetermined plan.

The ReSCUED Decision Matrix that you will find in Appendix A, brings the eight steps of strategy exploration to life. I recommend you take a moment to skim through the appendix to get a better sense of the process works, before returning here and continuing with your reading.

Creating the matrix is a revealing exercise of self-discovery. Imagine it's complete. You now revisit the matrix periodically and more often than the once-a-year offsite. The communication channels are open and bidirectional. Consider the following situations:

1. Customer support realizes from interaction with the end users that there's a new and more powerful way to create value for the customers. How is it prioritized?

2. Employees who attend a training course or trade show are conscious that the industry is evolving and that an additional threat is on the horizon. How does that get

considered?

3. The financial results show that one or more strategy initiatives are not working. What do you do with that information?

4. A few employees are having a coffee and discussing something they are working on. Together, they create the seed of a new idea. Does the idea die, or is there an avenue to get it adopted?

Set up a process and timeline for review meetings. Evaluate, consider, and score suggested initiatives. Reassessing, then adding, reordering, removing, or delaying items on the list.

The employees drinking coffee are an example of how innovation becomes real. They understand what the company is doing. The seed of an idea is a potential tactical delivery valued more by the customer, an original approach to solving a tactical challenge, or an idea that potentially drives a change in the strategic direction.

Invite those with ideas and suggestions to present at the strategy review. Recognize and reward innovation and ideas, even those that are not adopted.

Strategy exploration has given you a living and evolving document. You have defined what you do, who you do it for, and why the targeted customers choose you first. Most importantly, you have transformed 'strategic planning' into something that creates an agility your competitors will struggle to match.

I Have a Plan!

Spoiler Alert: He Didn't

As a product manager, I was still wet behind the ears, eager to prove myself in a company that wasn't thriving. We struggled with inconsistent revenue and only occasional profit. We were a company desperately searching for ideas to pull us out of the rut. When the Vice President of Engineering, Mark, burst into the boss's office one morning with an idea, his excitement was impossible to ignore.

"We need to have a meeting, now!" he barked, not slowing to explain. His enthusiasm was almost contagious, as if he'd stumbled upon the golden ticket that solved our problems. I grabbed my notebook and followed him to the conference room.

As we settled in, Mark wasted no time laying out his vision. "Formula One," he began, his eyes gleaming with excitement. "You know how several countries have implemented a ban on tobacco advertising? They can't have those logos on the cars anymore. No More Marlboro McClaren or Lotus John Player. Well, here's what we do: We model the Formula 1 tracks and the cars in 3D, as we do with our air traffic control simulators; then, during the TV broadcast in countries that permit tobacco advertising, we project the tobacco advertising onto the moving cars. Imagine it! The cars are speeding around the track, the logos on full display, as they're supposed to be."

I glanced at the VP of sales and marketing, who looked as surprised as I felt. Mark continued.

"We've got the experience. We build 3D models of airports, planes, and vehicles for our simulators, so it's another environment to model, right? And I've put together a team. They're ready to head to the F1 circuit (our office was a few miles from the Montreal track) to gather data and take photographs. We will have a prototype ready in no time!"

The room was silent momentarily, the weight of the idea settling. It was bold, sure, but it was plain that something was off. We barely kept our heads above water, struggling with the basics, such as consistent revenue and profit. My mind started churning through the logistics, the technical challenges, and the market implications. And the more I thought, the more this idea was not only way out of our league, it was ridiculous.

First, we weren't in the live broadcasting business. Our experience was limited to air traffic control simulators, which, while complex, had nothing to do with projecting live advertisements onto speeding cars. The technology needed for that differed from what we'd ever used. Even if we cobbled together a prototype, the chances of it working seamlessly in the chaotic, high-speed world of television and Formula 1 were slim to none.

Then there was the question of the market. Had anyone even considered whether this idea had a workable business model? Who are the customers? How big was the market for this technology? Was there enough demand to justify the investment? And who do we partner with? We hadn't researched or even dipped a toe in this industry's waters. Are we walking into a market that is too small to be profitable or dominated by companies that are far better equipped?

The more I thought, the more I realized we were so far out of our depth that I struggled to hold back my laughs. The VP was trying to solve our problems by chasing after something shiny and new without understanding what it took to succeed.

As the conversation in the room continued, with ideas bouncing back and forth, I knew I had to say something. Mark's enthusiasm was admirable, but it wasn't enough to make this pipe dream a reality.

Cutting through the noise, I said, "look, we're not in the live broadcasting business. The technology needed is way beyond our experience, and even if we build it, we'd need more research to understand the market and develop a business model that works. We're talking about a new industry with its challenges and competitors. We're setting ourselves up for failure and don't understand what's needed to succeed."

With the gravity of my words, the room fell silent. The boss nodded slowly, clearly thinking along the same lines. Mark's excitement dimmed, reality finally catching up.

Unsurprisingly, the project never left the room. It was more than obvious that we didn't have the skills, experience, or understanding to make it work, and pushing forward without those would be a costly mistake.

It was a harsh but necessary lesson. In our quest to find solutions to our revenue problems, we had to learn that not every idea, no matter how exciting, is worth pursuing. Sometimes, the most brilliant move is knowing when to walk away. If the VP of Engineering had run through an elementary version of 'roadblocks,' he would have realized his idea had no mileage.

From Crisis to Transformation

A Revolution in Organizational Alignment and Strategic Execution

The day started like any other at RAF Gütersloh. The familiar whine of aircraft jet engines and helicopter noises filled the air. This sound had become as natural as breathing to the men and women stationed there. But on May 6, 1988, the base heard that one of our Chinook helicopters had been involved in a major accident. ZA672 was taxiing into position for the Hannover airport airshow, its twin rotors spinning lazily in the morning light. In a moment of miscalculation, the massive helicopter blades struck the airport's passenger ramp with catastrophic force. The impact sent the Chinook into a violent roll, ending in a fireball that claimed the lives of three crew members and seriously injured another.

As the news came, a pall of disbelief settled over the base. The Chinook disaster didn't happen in isolation. It was the beginning of a disastrous summer. Over the next several months, more flight crews lost their lives in separate incidents. Others had come close, only saved by the Martin-Baker ejection seats. Each incident had been a blow, each investigation promising changes, yet the accidents continued to mount.

The string of tragedies had eroded morale and shaken confidence throughout the ranks. Whispers of systemic issues grew louder with each incident. The Royal Air Force had to confront the harsh truth: something was wrong.

In the aftermath, the Air Marshal knew he needed decisive action. This wasn't investigating a single incident anymore. It was addressing a pattern, a dangerous trend that threatened the very core of the RAF's operations and reputation.

The Air Marshall announced a visit to RAF Gütersloh. The news spread through the base. It was a signal of the gravity of the situation.

The atmosphere was thick with tension and anticipation as personnel gathered in the hangar. Pilots, ground crew, and support staff stood shoulder to shoulder, united in their grief and uncertainty.

When the Air Marshal took the podium, the hangar fell into a silence so complete you heard the distant whine of jet engines on the flight line.

"Ladies and gentlemen of RAF Gütersloh," he began, his voice carrying the weight of command and the burden of recent events, "I stand before you today not just as your Commanding Officer but as a fellow airman who shares in your pain and your concern for our future."

He paused, his gaze sweeping across the assembled faces. "The tragic losses of the past year are not another statistic. It is a stark reminder of the cost of our failures and the urgent need for change."

His words hung in the air, a frank acknowledgment of their crisis. "We've lost too many people. Each incident has wounded our organization, but together, they represent a systemic failure we will no longer ignore."

The Air Marshal then outlined a comprehensive strategy for change. It wasn't only new safety protocols or increased training. It was a fundamental culture shift, a realignment of the organization's core values and mission.

"From this day forward," he declared, his voice rising with conviction, "safety isn't only a procedure to be followed; it's the bedrock of everything we do. Excellence isn't an aspiration; it's our standard. And unity is our strength."

He spoke of increased accountability at every level, open communication channels, raising concerns without fear of reprisal, and a renewed focus on the human factors contributing to accidents.

"This change begins now and begins with each of you," he

concluded. "We are the Royal Air Force. We have faced greater challenges than this and emerged stronger. Together, we will honor the memory of those we've lost by building an RAF that is safer, more effective, and truer to its values."

As the Air Marshal stepped down from the podium, there was a shift in the room's energy. The grief and uncertainty remained, but determination ignited alongside them.

In the following weeks and months, RAF Gütersloh became the epicenter of a transformational wave. New training programs, overhauled communication protocols, and a proactive safety management culture took root.

The journey wasn't easy. Old habits died hard, and there were moments of doubt and setbacks. But gradually, the change became apparent. Incident rates dropped, morale improved, and a renewed sense of pride and purpose infused every aspect of operations.

One year after the Chinook tragedy, RAF Gütersloh had rebounded, it had become a model of operational excellence and safety. The turnaround served as a powerful reminder of what is achieved when an organization fully aligns itself with a strategy and shared purpose.

This story of RAF Gütersloh's transformation illustrates a crucial lesson for any organization facing crisis and change. In the business world, just as in the military, misalignment leads to catastrophic consequences. A strategy isn't a document to be filed away; it must be a living part of an organization's daily operations, understood and embraced by every member, from the highest levels of leadership to the front lines.

The RAF's journey from crisis to transformation shows that you overcome even the most daunting challenges with leadership, a well-defined strategy, and an unwavering commitment to change. It illustrates the power of organizational alignment in driving meaningful, lasting change.

Note, while the loss of lives and the events were real, I have taken liberty with the Air Marshal's dialog. This story took place 36 years ago, losing the details of the dialog to time, but the message was unambiguous.

DESTINATION THREE - CULTURE

Connecting Strategy and Execution with Culture

"Culture eats strategy for breakfast."–Peter Drucker.

Drucker's phrase emphasizes that while strategy is essential for providing direction and goals, culture is the engine that drives execution. A positive, cohesive culture enhances a strategy. A toxic or misaligned culture undermines even the best one.

While Peter Drucker's assertion that "culture eats strategy for breakfast" highlights the undeniable power of culture in shaping outcomes, culture and strategy are not separate or competing forces but as a symbiotic relationship. In a well-functioning organization, culture and strategy reinforce one another, driving performance and adaptability.

Business culture refers to the shared values, beliefs, behaviors, and practices that characterize the environment and operations within an organization. It influences how employees interact with one another and how the company approaches its challenges. Culture is the airspace you are flying through and the regulations that dictate what to do and how to do it. Culture is the foundation of performance and the catalyst for change. It drives people to act purposefully and adapt with resilience, making strategy a reality. It is the enabler for everything you do in value creation.

It is a set of conditions that, when considered as a whole, that determine the culture of the organization:

Performance

Culture is the operating system your employees run on. A positive culture? It's like upgrading everyone to the latest tech. A weak culture? You are asking them to work on Windows 95.

When culture aligns with goals, it's a tailwind. Everyone's pushing in the same direction; suddenly, those ambitious targets are not so far-fetched. A culture that embraces new ideas is a fertilizer for creativity. I've seen teams in stifling environments produce nothing but hot air while those given room to experiment, develop game-changers. And let's not forget accountability. In a strong culture, peer pressure becomes your ally. No one aspires to be the weak link, and that drive pushes performance across the board. It's having an army of self-motivated overachievers, minus the ego clashes.

Well-being, More Than Just Yoga Classes

Employee well-being isn't a nice-to-have; it's a must-have. And no, I'm not talking about installing a meditation room and calling it a day. A toxic culture is like a pressure cooker. It produces results in the short term, but eventually, it'll blow up in your face. A supportive one acts as a pressure release valve, keeping your team sane and productive.

What about work-life balance? If you glorify 80-hour weeks, you're not getting heroes but breeding burnouts. Balance isn't a weakness; it's sustainability. It's the contrast between a marathon runner and a sprinter who collapses after 100 meters. And while we're at it, let's discuss the elephant in the room: mental health. Stigmatizing mental health issues is like ignoring a check engine light. It's fine now, but you're headed for a breakdown. Trust me, I've seen it happen, and it's not pretty.

Engagement: What Separates a Job and a Mission

Engagement is an environment where people give a damn. You've struck gold if you connect daily tasks to a bigger purpose. People work harder when they believe in what they're doing. They are not building a wall; they are building a cathedral.

But purpose alone isn't enough. Appreciation is fuel for your team's motivation. And no, I don't mean participation trophies, genuine recognition for genuine achievements. It's incredible how far a sincere "good job" goes. Pair that with a company that promotes learning and development, and you're not filling roles; you're building careers. And trust me, loyalty follows. It separates the employees who constantly check the time, eager for the workday to end, from those absorbed in their tasks for where hours pass unnoticed.

Culture isn't a fluffy concept for HR to worry about. It's the backbone of your organization, the invisible force that turns a group of individuals into a high-performing team. Get it right, and everything else falls into place. Get it wrong, and... well, let's say you'll wonder why your brilliant strategies aren't working out.

A strong business culture enhances employee satisfaction, attracts top talent, and improves overall performance. Conversely, a toxic or poorly defined culture leads to high turnover and hinders a company's success. It is never a set-it-and-forget-it. People come and go. Business conditions change. Employee expectations evolve. Stakeholders make new demands. These will eat away at your culture, which needs to be reset. Cultural evolution is not discrete. It's a living part of your business.

Endless online articles recommend how to turn around a company's poor culture. You understand that leadership, organizational structure, and people are vital components. I don't intend to regurgitate that advice. I will emphasize the importance of examining this topic in greater detail.

However, I will share my advice on four components, without which making a meaningful change will be impossible: communication, values, performance, and arguably, the most importantly, purpose.

The Tenerife Disaster

A Failure to Communicate

The tranquil beauty of Tenerife, a jewel in the Canary Islands, was shattered on a foggy March 27th, 1977. Los Rodeos Airport, a bustling gateway to paradise, became the scene of the deadliest accident in aviation history. Destined for a collision were two Boeing 747s, KLM Flight 4805 and Pan Am Flight 1736, their paths entangled in a deadly dance of miscommunication and the unforgiving veil of fog.

A terrorist attack at Gran Canaria airport had earlier forced the diversion of many flights to the smaller Los Rodeos. The airport, unprepared for such an influx, became congested, with planes lining the runways like stranded giants. Among them were the KLM and Pan Am 747s, both unknowingly waiting for their fateful encounter.

The fog, a thick, relentless blanket, descended upon the airport, shrouding the tarmac in a ghostly gray. Visibility dropped drastically, making navigation treacherous. Communication between the control tower and the planes became a struggle, garbled messages fighting against the radio static and urgency.

Captain Jacob Veldhuyzen van Zanten, a veteran pilot with a meticulous reputation commanding the KLM flight, was eager to leave. He thought he had received clearance for takeoff, a misunderstanding fueled by the dense fog and the pressure to resume their journey.

Meanwhile, following instructions from the control tower, Captain Victor Grubbs of Pan Am Flight 1736 taxied his plane along the fog-obscured runway. Unbeknownst to him, the KLM 747, eager to escape the delay, was beginning its takeoff roll a few hundred meters ahead.

In a heart-stopping moment, the KLM Boeing roared to life, its powerful engines pushing it forward into the dense fog. The static and confusion garbled and delayed a desperate warning from the control tower urging an abort. It was too late.

The Pan Am 747, still taxiing on the runway, was struck with unimaginable force. The impact, a loud explosion of metal and shattered glass, ripped through the quiet of the morning. Fire, a monstrous inferno, erupted, consuming the two giants of the sky.

The fog, a cruel accomplice, initially hid the carnage from view. The billowing smoke, dark against the gray sky, soon betrayed the horrifying scene. Screams echoed through the air, a harrowing symphony of terror and despair.

The world watched in horror as the news of the tragedy unfolded. The Tenerife Airport disaster claimed 583 lives, a staggering toll that shook the world and left an indelible mark on aviation history. Only 61 souls survived the Pan Am crash, the tales a chilling reminder of the fragility of life.

Poor Communication and Disaster

A Correlation

There is no better example of the impact of communication on an organization than the Tenerife airport disaster.

The KLM crew exhibited a steep authority gradient. In this cultural issue, subordinates feel unable to challenge the decisions of their superiors. Despite the confusion and uncertainty, the first officer and flight engineer did not effectively challenge the captain's premature takeoff decision. This deference to authority was a leading contributor to the accident.

Aviation culture often discouraged junior crew members from questioning a captain's actions. The outcome would have been different if the cockpit culture had been more open to cross-checking and challenging decisions.

The crews were under pressure because of the diversion to Tenerife, caused by a bomb threat at their original destination. Stress was exacerbated by the time pressure to meet duty regulations. This highlights how the culture of dealing with stress and time constraints in aviation impacts decision-making.

The inquest found several other factors that contributed to this catastrophic event.

1. The KLM crew misinterpreted the ATC route clearance as permission to take-off.

2. Radio interference prevented regular communication between the control tower, the KLM, and the Pan Am planes.

3. The KLM captain began the takeoff without clearance from ATC.

4. Diverted flights to Los Rodeos, an airport not equipped to manage such traffic, led to crowded taxiways and non-standard procedures.

5. Non-standard terminology in radio communications contributed to misunderstandings.

At its core, the Tenerife disaster was a breakdown in communication. Misunderstandings, assumptions, and a failure to verify information led to a series of decisions that culminated in the loss of life. What happened that day shows the cascading effect of communication breakdowns. What began as a series of minor misunderstandings culminated in a catastrophic event.

After the Tenerife disaster, the aviation industry underwent a cultural shift, leading to the development of Crew Resource Management (CRM), which promotes:

- Open communication between every member of the cockpit, regardless of rank.

- Encouragement for junior officers to challenge or question decisions when necessary.

- Training on recognizing the importance of interpersonal dynamics and mitigating the authority gradient.

CRM has since become a cornerstone of aviation safety culture.

The Tenerife disaster is a case study of the central role of unambiguous, verified, and open communication. By internalizing these lessons, corporate leaders can build more resilient and efficient organizational communication systems. In doing so, they mitigate risks and create an environment where information flows and decisions are well-informed, aligning the entire organization toward common goals.

CORPORATE COMMUNICATIONS

The Invisible Force

Corporate communication isn't flooding inboxes or hosting endless meetings. It's the invisible force that will transform a bunch of employees into a high-performing team or your grand strategy into a sad joke taped to the break room wall.

Communication is the central nervous system of your organization. Your strategy? That's the brain. Your employees? The muscles. But without communication, you've got a body that can't coordinate its movements. You end up with a corporate version of the chicken dance instead of a synchronized swim team.

In my years leading through highs and lows, I've witnessed how communication strengthens or weakens a culture. Get it right, and you will work with seamless efficiency. The group operates with a unified purpose and coordinated action. Get it wrong, and you're overseeing a corporate version of a middle school dance: awkward, disorganized, and with everyone hugging the walls.

Executives often treat communication as the corporate equivalent of small talk at a cocktail party. Nice to have, but not essential. They are mistaken. Communication keeps people informed and creates a shared reality, aligning goals and a sense of belonging.

Silence isn't golden; it's a missed opportunity. Let's learn how to make a noise that matters.

Tenerife is a stark reminder of the necessity of unambiguous communication. While the tragedy occurred in the aviation industry, its lessons resonate powerfully in the corporate world, offering valuable insights for business leaders and communication professionals.

One lesson is the danger of assumed understanding. In corporate settings, this translates to the essential nature of clarity and confirmation in communications.

Take this example from my early days as a CEO. I agreed to sell our marketing demonstration simulator to a customer who did not have the budget to buy a new system. We saw this as an opportunity to subsidize the upgrade to a more impressive demonstrator. The employees? Well, one or two saw it as evidence that we were struggling financially, and before too long, the rumor had cascaded into a belief that the company was heading for bankruptcy and their jobs were at risk. I took immediate action to quell the rumor and end the unrest. I gathered the employees and explained not only the truth about the sale, but also about the dangers of unchecked rumors. The company could have prevented the situation if employees had felt empowered to ask questions or, more importantly, if management, myself included, had communicated its intentions.

In the corporate world, 'fog' takes many forms: market uncertainties, incomplete data, or rapid changes in the business landscape. Communicators must navigate these challenges, conveying information clearly despite external pressures or limitations.

Non-standard terminology underscores the weight of establishing and adhering to communication protocols in business settings. Whether it's standardized reporting formats, consistent terminology in project management, or defined escalation procedures, establishing communication norms prevents misunderstandings and ensures efficiency.

Corporate leaders must view communication challenges as opportunities for systemic improvement. This is the reality of the interconnected nature of organizational messaging. A minor miscommunication in one department, or more worryingly from a position of authority, has far-reaching consequences across the entire organization.

Make sure that messages are understood as intended, whether they are a major decision or a routine communication.

A Corporate Communication Lesson

The Self-Inflicted wound

Surely, the CEO of a company worth millions understands how to be an effective communicator? Well, let me share a true story.

It was the day the company imploded. I accompanied our CEO to an all-hands meeting at one of our international facilities. It was supposed to be a routine visit, a chance to boost morale and align our global teams. Instead, it turned into a masterclass in how not to communicate.

Our CEO had been on a data-gathering mission for months, obsessed with productivity metrics. He'd collected numbers on everything from direct hours booked to sick leave taken. I should have seen the warning signs when he spent the entire flight poring over spreadsheets, muttering about percentages and ratios.

The CEO strode to the front of an overfilled break room, chest puffed out, armed with his data. Without so much as a "hello" or "thank you for having me," he launched into his speech. "I've been analyzing the numbers," he declared, his voice echoing through the silent room, "and I have to say, the U.S. office is more productive than this office." Paraphrasing for effect, this accurately conveys what the gathered employees heard.

I watched the sea of faces shift from anticipation to confusion to disbelief. But our fearless leader wasn't done. He rattled off statistics, each a dagger to the room's morale. I wanted to sink into my chair or disappear entirely.

As if sensing the growing tension, the CEO delivered his coup de grâce. "Things have to change," he announced, his voice hard. "And if you don't like it, you can work elsewhere."

The silence that followed was deafening.

As we hastily exited the auditorium, dodging glares and whispered comments, I realized the size of the CEO's blunder. In his quest for data-driven decision-making, he'd missed the forest for the trees.

He didn't consider that our offices had different roles. The international office focused on software engineering and the U.S. office handled installations and customer services. He'd ignored the different compensation, benefits, and vacation disparities, and he was oblivious to the differences in culture and approaches to work-life balance. This office had employees from over 20 countries, most non-native English speakers. In short, he'd compared apples to oranges and then criticized the oranges for not being apple-y enough.

The fallout was immediate and lasting. Employee satisfaction plummeted, productivity took a nosedive, and we lost some of our best talent in the following months. The lingering consequences of this presentation echoed throughout the organization for years.

It was a harsh lesson in context and the role of empathetic, thoughtful communication. Numbers tell a story, but they rarely tell the entire story. And even when the numbers suggest harsh changes, how you communicate those changes is important.

To this day, whenever I see a CEO armed with a PowerPoint full of graphs and a gleam in their eyes, I get nervous. Sometimes, I want to say, "Before you start, let me tell you a story about an all-hands meeting that made 'The Office' look like a feel-good documentary."

A Bonus Communication Lesson

Seniority Changes the Message

As I ascended the corporate ladder, a perplexing pattern appeared. My teams misinterpreted my once transparent and collaborative communications. The higher I climbed, the more my words morphed into something unintended, creating confusion and misalignment. I had come from air traffic control that used words sparingly and precisely chosen to avoid the potential for ambiguity and misunderstanding; It made little sense to me.

I tried everything. I meticulously articulated my thoughts, ensuring each sentence was unambiguous and precise. I even prefaced my opinions with phrases such as, "Just my two cents" or "Here's an idea to consider." Sacrilegious, at least to me, I even questioned if my Scottish brogue was a contributing (of course, it wasn't) or if I had subconsciously slipped into speaking Martian. It had gotten to where I started each meeting with a blunt statement, "We are here to discuss and share ideas and opinions. If what I say is an instruction, I will explicitly tell you it's an instruction." Yet, the misinterpretations persisted, leaving me baffled and frustrated.

During a casual conversation with a small team, I inquired about a recent decision and was curious about the approach. The response was simple: "Because you said so."

It hit me like a thunderbolt. Once welcomed as contributions, my enthusiastic expressions of opinion were now perceived as directives. My seniority had inadvertently transformed my words into commands, stifling open dialogue and creative thinking.

The realization was both humbling and enlightening. It underscored the profound impact of hierarchical power on communication dynamics. The higher your position, the more weight your words carry, regardless of your intent. You might believe you are offering a casual suggestion as a peer, but often it is interpreted as an order.

This experience taught me the indispensability of mindful communication, especially in leadership roles. It's not what you say but how it's perceived. It's creating a safe space for open dialogue and empowering team members to share their ideas without fear of misinterpretation or reprisal.

Words are not necessarily what sends the message. Format, tone, volume, and body language communicate much more than any words you use.

Seniority changes the game. Your words, once harmless pebbles, become boulders, shaping the landscape of your team's understanding. As a leader, it's your responsibility to wield this power with care.

One last consideration, the reader's mood sets your tone when you use a written form. That email you wrote while enjoying your morning coffee, that is asking for help is perceived easily as an aggressive demand if the recipient had a frustrating drive into the office. If in doubt, pick up the phone.

Fog, Fumes, and Faith

Another Tale from RAF Gutersloh

It was 1989, and I was an inexperienced first tour controller stationed at RAF Gutersloh, a mere two-hour drive from the East German border. A thick fog had descended upon the airfield. Visibility was zero, and we were closed for business.

I was lounging in the radar room, feet propped up on the console, engrossed in a dog-eared paperback, and drinking NATO standard tea (milk and two sugars). The loudest sound was the low hum of electronics from the radar equipment. Hunching over the desk, Dave, our seasoned supervisor, was wrestling with the endless paperwork.

The rest of our merry band had retreated to the adjacent ready room. The aroma of strong coffee wafted through the air, mingling with the banter and laughter that filtered through the door.

It was, in short, a perfectly ordinary, mind-numbingly dull day.

Until it wasn't.

The sudden sound of the telephone shattered the tranquility. The blinking light on the console showed it was clutch radar, the German upper airspace unit. Dave casually donned his headset and selected the line, answering simply, "Gutersloh." Dave's head snapped up; paperwork forgotten. I only heard one side of the conversation. "But we have zero visibility," Dave said. I nearly fell out of my chair; I sensed something was wrong.

Snapping his fingers, he said, "Get the others."

I sprinted to the break room, words tumbling out in a rush of adrenaline and urgency. Mugs clattered on the table; my colleagues leaped into action, any trace of relaxation evaporating instantly.

Back in the radar room, we fell into a well-rehearsed dance. Training kicked in, and muscle memory took over as we manned our stations. The supervisor's voice was unambiguous and authoritative, assigning roles and responsibilities. In an instant, the room transformed from a sleepy outpost to a hive of frenzied activity.

"Contact, Two eight, two, two, five," Dave said, accepting responsibility for the F16s as he relayed the approach controller's frequency.

"We have eleven Belgian F-16s inbound. Fuel emergency". Dave barked, his voice calm but edged with steel. From our training, we learned not to make pointless visibility comments. Dave understood.

The approach control frequency came to life. "Gutersloh, Mission flight, eleven F16s with you. We are a fuel emergency." The lead pilot transmitted in a strong French accent.

"Radar contact, turn right, heading zero, nine zero," the approach controller instructed.

"Keep it tight, Gutersloh; we only have one shot." The pilot came back.

Dave selected the direct line to the tower. "Tower, turn on the runway lights, max brightness he ordered, and get the emergency teams moving." Without waiting for acknowledgment, Dave passed on the details of the incoming emergency.

The tower controller relayed the conversation to the duty pilot, ground controller, and assistant while picking up the red emergency phone. Waiting for the panel lights to show that medical, fire, and operations had picked up and were listening, "Eleven F16's fuel emergency inbound runway two seven. Rendezvous point Alpha 7, " He said, passing the coordinates for the runway intersection. Hanging up the phone, he repeated the message on the station-wide broadcast, alerting everyone on base.

Back in the radar room, bathed in darkness except for the faint orange glow of the radar displays, the approach controller began the vectors, setting up the formation for transfer to the radar director.

Typically, the radar director separates the formation into individual callsigns, sequencing them for an eight-mile final approach, in a three to five-mile trail to keep them a safe distance apart. Eleven planes were too much for one Radar Director, and an 8-mile final and 5-mile trail wouldn't cut it.

Everyone in the room understood the mix of radio transmissions, telephone calls, and conversations, unintelligible to a casual observer.

"They are running on fumes. I want a short pattern. Aim for a 3-mile intercept and a 1-mile separation on final approach, " the supervisor instructed.

What followed was a symphony of controlled chaos. Our voices intertwined in a complex melody of instructions, acknowledgments, and vital information. The fog blinded us, but our radar became our eyes, cutting through the murk with electronic precision.

My assigned role that morning was one of the two precision approach radar (PAR) positions. The PAR controller adjusts two narrow radar beams to look up and out into the final approach to 'talk down' the pilot with precise heading and descent rate instructions.

The radar screen showed two views: the plane's position above or below the best glide path and the position left or right of the runway approach track. The pilot received guidance relative to his height and heading every mile until the 5-mile marker and then every half mile. It's straightforward...on a typical day.

But today was not typical. With a one-mile separation, it needed two PAR controllers. Instead of one plane on a single frequency, a short pattern meant alternating so that each position controlled two planes on a single frequency, something I had never experienced. The narrow radar antennas added to the complexity. One of the PAR controllers uses a joystick to adjust the position of both antennas to optimize the signal. To track two planes, let alone 3 or 4, is challenging. If any plane fell outside the antenna signal, it disappeared.

We knew we had to get this right. Without the fuel to make a second attempt, an aborted approach undoubtedly meant an ejection with injuries to the pilot and a mangled plane somewhere a few miles from the airfield.

These planes were doing at least 160 knots, so a mile passed quickly, and every half mile was even quicker. I sounded like an auctioneer at a cattle market. "Mission One, six miles, slightly left of centerline correcting. Mission Four, 12 miles, turn right 5 degrees, well left of centerline, not correcting. Mission One, 5 miles, begin descent now for a 3-degree flight path."

The critical moment was the pilot's MDH, or minimum descent height, about 200 feet above the touchdown. If the pilot did not see the runway lights at the MDH, they regulations state they must abort. It is also where the controllers end the service.

"Mission One, approaching minimum descent height, on glide path on centerline; passing minimum descent height, radar service terminated."

"Keep talking," came the impossibly calm voice of the first F16 pilot. "On glide path, on the centerline," I continued. over touchdown now."

I held my breath. After a few seconds, the pilot said, "Thank you, Gutersloh." I let out my breath, knowing those three words conveyed much more than a simple thank you. It was fighter pilot speak, for I owe your team a beer. I turned my attention to the following plane and replied, "Keep rolling." The next one is right behind.

The minutes stretched like hours as we guided each plane through the fog. Every command had to be perfect, and every calculation was precise. There was zero margin for error.

We brought them in one by one. Each successful landing was a minor victory, a life saved. But we couldn't celebrate until eleven F16s were on the ground.

The last three fighters were running on vapors, their fuel gauges flirting with empty. As they rolled out from the landing, their engines sputtered and died. The planes stopped on the runway. The ground crew had to tow them to the parking apron, but they were safe.

As the adrenaline ebbed, I looked around the room at my colleagues. Exhausted but wearing expressions of fierce pride. We had done it.

At that moment, I understood the actual value of what we did. It wasn't about the technology, processes, and protocols. The people, trained, dedicated, and working together as a seamless unit, made the difference. It was about trust in each other and our systems, forged through countless hours of preparation for such moments.

Eleven pilots, eleven planes, safe.

As I finally allowed myself to slump back in my chair, I knew I'd remember this day for the rest of my life, not only as a tale of fog, fumes, and near-disaster averted but as a testament to the power of people, training, systems, and processes in perfect harmony.

The paperback I'd been reading lay forgotten on the console. Once again, silence settled over the radar room. I stood up, my tea now cold. "Who wants a brew?" I called out as I walked to the ready room. "Tea NATO standard," Dave responded, now back at his desk reading papers as if nothing had happened.

VALUES, PERFORMANCE, AND PURPOSE

Driving Business Excellence

The story of guiding Belgian F-16s through zero visibility isn't only a tale of aeronautical prowess. It illustrates how values, performance, and purpose drive culture and value creation.

Let's start with values. When that emergency call came in, our team didn't hesitate. We sprang into action, not because it was in our job description, but because saving lives was a core value. In business, we often speak of values like integrity and excellence. But controllers embody those values. We didn't need motivational posters; our values were intrinsic to who we were and how we operated.

Now, consider performance. Under immense pressure, we didn't manage; we excelled. This wasn't following a predetermined script. It was adapting rapidly, making split-second decisions, and executing precisely. In the business world, we sometimes conflate busy-ness with performance. But performance is about delivering results when the stakes are highest.

And then there's purpose. Controllers aren't merely directing air traffic. They preserve lives. Every instruction and every calculation had this higher purpose. In business, we get so focused on financial metrics that we lose sight of our greater mission. But extraordinary things happen when a genuine purpose drives a team.

Here's where it converges. Values, performance, and purpose aren't lofty ideals for corporate mission statements. They're the foundation of business value creation.

Consider this: Decision-making becomes consistent when your team aligns around core values. You don't need to micromanage because everyone understands what's expected.

That's operational efficiency, and it directly drives value.

When your team performs at this level, you're not meeting expectations; you're surpassing them. This caliber of performance builds reputation, fosters customer loyalty, and expands market share. These factors translate directly to business value.

The purpose is the catalyst that energizes it. When your team genuinely believes in what they're doing, they'll innovate, go above and beyond, and solve problems proactively. This is how you create enduring value.

Crucially, you can't manufacture this. You can't declare values, set performance indicators, and craft a purpose statement. It must be authentic and lived daily, like those controllers in that radar room.

While most businesses aren't dealing with life-or-death scenarios like guiding fuel-depleted fighters through zero visibility, the principles stay the same. When your values are unshakeable, your performance is exceptional, and your purpose is clear and compelling, you're creating business value and redefining what's possible in your industry.

As you develop your business strategy, look beyond market share and profit margins. Consider the values that will guide your decisions in challenging times. Reflect on how you'll perform when it truly matters. And most importantly, define the purpose that will inspire your team to give their best daily.

Spreadsheets and presentations don't create business value. People create it. People with strong values, exceptional performance, and a compelling reason for their work. That's the essence of sustainable business success. Everything else is secondary. Let's look at values, performance, and purpose in more detail.

Values

We Do What We Say We Do

It's time to discuss something often overlooked (or deliberately minimized) in strategy, performance, and culture discussions. Values.

"Values? Isn't that feel-good corporate speak? How does that relate to ROI or market share?" Your company's values are far more than words on a wall or in an employee handbook. They are the clandestine dynamo of value creation.

When properly understood and used, values become the framework for decision-making in your organization. They're not only ethics or corporate social responsibility, though those are important. They establish a shared understanding of what matters most, acceptable trade-offs, and which behaviors earn rewards. Think about it. In a fast-moving business, we waste time when employees are unsure about the right action. How often do different departments work at cross-purposes because they refine for other priorities?

Your values shape your organization, which drives performance. A study by Deloitte found that 94% of executives and 88% of employees think a distinct workplace culture is essential to business success. And what shapes culture more than the values you uphold?

Values play a role in talent management. In a competitive job market, top talent isn't looking for a paycheck but a purpose. When your values resonate with employees, you create engagement and commitment that no number of perks or bonuses buy.

Values reduce hiring costs and improve retention. Zappos gives an example. They famously offered new hires $2,000 to quit after their first week of training. Why? Because they only want employees who buy into their values. It's a short-term cost that pays massive dividends in the long run.

Some of you think, "This sounds great in theory, but how do we measure it? How do we know if our values are creating value?"

This is an excellent question. The key is to integrate your values into your performance metrics. If innovation is a core value, track the number of new ideas generated and implemented. If sustainability is important, include environmental impact in your performance evaluations. Incorporate peer feedback into your reviews.

By doing this, you send a message: our values aren't nice-to-haves; they're must-haves. They're an integral part of how we define and measure success.

I want to challenge you to think differently about your company's values. Create a more focused and aligned organization. They're about attracting and keeping the best talent and making better decisions faster. In short, they're creating value. I urge you to take a fresh look at your values. Are they defined? Are the values reflected in your decision-making processes, organizational structure, and performance metrics? If not, you're leaving value on the table.

Performance

Building a High-performance Culture

A high-performance culture transforms good organizations into great ones. The intangible energy pulses through the hallways, the shared sense of purpose that lights up people's eyes, and the collective drive that turns ambitious goals into reality.

> "Individual commitment to a group effort - that makes a team work, a company work, a society work, a civilization work." - Vince Lombardi

A cohesive team is more than a group of individuals working towards a common goal; it's a synergistic unit where the whole is greater than the sum of its parts. Assembling talent is the beginning. Building a team begins with bringing together individuals with complementary skills and diverse perspectives. Trust lies at the heart of this. Not the flimsy kind that crumbles at the first sign of trouble, but a robust, resilient trust that empowers people to take risks, speak their minds, and push boundaries.

Trust builds everything in a high-performance organization.

Hand in hand with trust comes autonomy. Allowing people to own their work, decide, stumble, and learn. Avoid treating employees as cogs in a machine and value them as creative and capable individuals. When you trust people to do their jobs, they exceed expectations in ways that rigid control never allows.

Open communication flows through high-performance teams. It avoids top-down missives or corporate speech. It's an honest dialogue. Leaders who listen as much as they talk, teams that debate ideas vigorously but respectfully, and give constructive feedback.

Embedded learning makes mistakes a growth opportunity, not causes for punishment. A hunger for knowledge and a restless curiosity drive continuous improvement. From formal training programs to informal mentoring, the organization hums with the energy of people expanding their skills and horizons.

Recognition goes beyond annual bonuses or employee-of-the-month plaques. Recognition comes from a place of appreciation where you notice and celebrate great work in real-time. Understand that a well-timed word of praise, especially if it is public, is as motivating as a monetary reward. Showcasing effort and progress, alongside outcomes, encourages sustained growth and engagement.

Leadership in this environment is less command and control and more inspiration and empowerment. Leaders set the tone, embodying the values they espouse and nurturing the talents of those around them. They're coaches and facilitators, removing obstacles and creating the conditions for their teams to excel.

Building such a culture is no small feat. Unwavering commitment, consistent action, and, often, a willingness to make tough decisions are structural.

However, the rewards are immense. Imagine a workplace humming with electric energy, people so absorbed in their craft that they forget to check the clock. Here, ideas spark and catch fire. Colleagues feed off each other's energy, pushing boundaries and shattering expectations. It's not work; it's a mission, with everyone all in.

Purpose

$110 million or Bust

A few weeks after arriving in Montreal from the UK, I stood in the barren expanse of the second floor of the office building, a fitting metaphor for the task ahead - a vast emptiness waiting to be filled with sweat, tears, and profanity. The CEO had convinced me to up sticks and travel thousands of miles on the promise of a product manager job and a product and company poised to win a game-changing contract. It didn't take long to discover that the CEO had spun me a yarn, and I fell for it.

The customer demonstration and evaluation for the game-changing contract were only 4-months away. It was time to do my best MacGuyver act and see what we could pull together from the existing pieces and judicious software development.

"Right then," I announced to the eager faces of my newly formed tiger team, my Scottish brogue echoing in the space. "Welcome to 'Mission Impossible: Air Traffic Control Edition.' Our task is to turn two wheezing geriatric pieces of software into an ultramodern simulator in four months. No pressure, eh?"

The team stared at me with excitement and terror in their eyes. I was feeling the same cocktail of emotions myself.

"Now, I know what you're thinking," I said, my tone dripping with sarcasm. "Why take eighteen months when we can cram into four? Let's say our CEO has a unique understanding of time management. But fear not; we will make it happen even if it kills us. Which, by the way, is a distinct possibility."

And so began our four-month odyssey. We transformed that empty floor into a hive of activity fueled by an unholy trinity of caffeine, determination, and the constant fear of failure.

Whiteboards sprouted from every available surface, covered in a mixture of code, diagrams, and the occasional doodle (I maintain that my stick figure representation of the CEO was exact and tasteful).

The team worked with an enthusiasm I'd never seen. We became a tight-knit group, a slightly dysfunctional, perpetually exhausted group. We celebrated minor victories and mourned setbacks with group therapy sessions disguised as pizza parties.

One particularly memorable night, as we lay sprawled across various surfaces, requirements swimming before our tired eyes, our resident genius, Daniel, shot up suddenly.

"I've got it!" he said.

We stared at him, waiting.

"Well?" I prompted. "Don't keep us in suspense. Have you discovered the secret to time travel? Because that's the only thing that'll save us now."

Daniel grinned sheepishly. "No, but I have found a bug in old spaghetti code, causing our repeated software crashes."

In our sleep-deprived state, this felt like winning the lottery.

Of course, it wasn't smooth sailing. The CEO and other executives often offered to 'help' with suggestions that were about as helpful as a single malt whisky at an AA meeting. I became the team's bouncer, deflecting these well-meaning but disruptive interventions with a combination of Scottish charm and thinly veiled threats.

"Ah, Mr. CEO," I'd say, intercepting him before he entered our lair. "Unless you tell us you've added more hours to the day, we're too busy to entertain visitors. But you are free to leave a message with my secretary." I'd gesture to the potted plant named Gladys.

Against the odds, we did it. Four months of blood, sweat, and tears later (and, in one memorable instance, a small fire), we transformed our aging software into a cutting-edge simulator that blew the competition out of the water.

Six months after we began, we stood together, watching the VP of sales and marketing announce our contract win; amid popping champagne corks, I felt a surge of pride unlike anything I'd experienced. This was a professional victory and a testament to what people achieve when united by a common goal and a touch of shared insanity.

"Well done, team," I said, my voice gruff with emotion. "We've proved that the impossible is possible, provided you have enough coffee and a blatant disregard for work-life balance."

We laughed, we cried, and we fell asleep standing up. But most importantly, we had shown that with the right people, motivation, and perhaps a splash of Scottish sarcasm, there's no limit, even if it means occasionally sleeping under your desk and forgetting what daylight looks like.

The Purpose of Purpose

The Truth Behind Performance

Why did this team move mountains? Why did they sacrifice sleep, social lives, and sanity to meet an insane deadline? It wasn't for the money, though the bonus checks were a pleasant touch.

No, what drove this team to the brink of madness and back was something far more powerful: purpose.

Every single member of that tiger team volunteered for this suicide mission. They weren't volun-told or coerced. Employees applied for a place on the team. They interviewed and fought for the chance to be part of something bigger than themselves. Folks itching to prove their mettle flooded me with applications when I put out the call.

These people willingly signed up for 18-hour days, 7 days a week, for four months. They knew what they were getting into. A pressure cooker environment with an immovable deadline looming over their heads. And they jumped in headfirst.

Why? Because we built a culture of purpose.

I emphasized from the start that this was about more than winning a contract. This was revolutionizing air traffic control training. It was pushing the boundaries of what was possible in our field. We weren't coding; we were changing the game.

This sense of purpose became our north star. It guided every decision, fueled every late-night coding session, and kept us going when caffeine and sheer stubbornness weren't enough.

We created a culture where every team member felt ownership of the mission. They were players in a high-stakes game where their ideas mattered. We recognized their efforts, and I shared their struggles.

In that empty office space, we built more than a product. We built a tribe united by a common goal. A family bonded by shared hardships and victories. A team that knew, to their core, that what they were doing mattered.

This is the power of culture. It's not ping-pong tables or casual Fridays. It's creating an environment where people find meaning in their work, connecting to something larger than themselves. It's about where they're willing to go to the mat for their teammates and a shared vision.

In those four months, I learned a lesson I never forgot: culture and purpose aren't HR buzzwords. They are the secret weapon that turns the impossible into reality. It's what makes people willingly sacrifice their comfort for a shot at greatness.

Do you want to create real value in your business? Start with your culture. Give your people a purpose worth fighting for. Create an environment where they do the best work of their lives. Do that, and you'll be amazed at what they achieve.

Because it's not the money, it's not the accolades. It's being part of something meaningful. Something transformative. Something that makes the blood, sweat, and tears worth it.

That culture turns a ragtag and diverse group of coders into world-beaters. And that's the culture that makes your business unstoppable.

Destination Four - Urgency

The Enemy of Complacency

Success breeds complacency. I've seen it repeatedly: companies riding high on their wins, patting themselves on the back, thinking they've cracked the code. "We're crushing it. Revenues were up 30% last year, so why change?" That mindset is a one-way ticket to obsolescence.

The market doesn't give a damn about your past glories. Yesterday's groundbreaking innovation is today's table stakes. I've seen industry leaders topple because they got too comfortable and slow while hungrier, faster-moving upstarts ate their lunch.

Urgency in execution isn't a nice-to-have. Countless brilliant strategies have withered on the vine because teams lacked the fire in their belly to drive them home.

In my years in the trenches, one truth has become unmistakable: the business graveyard is littered with companies with powerful ideas but no urgency; here's looking at you, Blackberry and Nokia. Once-successful firms that were lulled into a false sense of security by their success. They took their foot off the gas, thinking momentum was enough to carry them forward indefinitely. Spoiler alert: it doesn't.

The market waits for no one. Your competitors aren't sitting on their hands, and neither are your customers. The instant you stop pushing, you lose ground.

Do you want an example?

Artificial Intelligence has changed market dynamics, ushering in unprecedented change and innovation. AI isn't another tool in the corporate arsenal; it's a paradigm shift rewriting the rules of competition and transforming the competitive arena. What once took years to develop is now prototyped in hours. Market research that used to need months of surveys and focus groups is now conducted in real-time, with AI analyzing vast troves of data to uncover insights at lightning speed.

This acceleration isn't linear; it's exponential. As AI systems become more sophisticated, they're not only speeding up existing processes, but they make entirely new business models and revenue streams possible. The pace of change is no longer measured in years or even months, but in weeks and days. Companies that were industry leaders five years ago now struggle to keep up with AI-powered startups that iterate and pivot with breathtaking agility. This relentless acceleration forces businesses to rethink everything from product development cycles to organizational structures. The traditional five-year plan is obsolete as soon as it's written. In this AI-driven landscape, adaptability is a prerequisite for survival. As AI continues to evolve, incorporating advances in machine learning, natural language processing, and predictive analytics, the pace of change will speed up even further, challenging our notions of what's possible.

Urgency turns strategy from a boardroom PowerPoint into cold, hard results. It's the difference between "We'll get to it" and "We're making this happen now." When your team operates with a sense of urgency, mountains move. Seemingly insurmountable obstacles become speed bumps.

Urgency isn't running around aimlessly. It's focused and relentless forward motion. It's making quick decisions, learning from mistakes, and pivoting on a dime when needed.

In the cockpit of a business, urgency is your afterburner. It's what you kick in when you need to outmaneuver a competitor, seize a fleeting market opportunity, or pull out of a nosedive. Companies can triple their market share in months, not years, when they cranked up the urgency dial.

Urgency is contagious. When leaders model it, teams catch fire. Entire organizations transform from sluggish bureaucracies to nimble powerhouses when urgency became part of their DNA.

But Urgency without clear direction leads to wasted effort. It needs to be channeled and focused. Every person in your organization must wake up with a sense of what needs to be done today to move the needle.

Culture plays a massive role here. You can't mandate urgency. Cultivate it by creating an environment that empowers people to act and that values urgency. Where 'good enough' and 'we've always done it this way' are dirty phrases.

Nothing kills urgency faster than bureaucracy and fear of failure. Arriving at a new job, I discovered that the purchase of my laptop, without which I couldn't do my job, needed approval by the management committee and six signatures, including from the CFO and CEO.

Strip away unnecessary layers of approval. Create safe spaces for calculated risks. Celebrate quick wins and learn from setbacks without pointing fingers.

You can't make more time. Every day without progress is when your competition is gaining ground. Urgency isn't panic or stress, it's respect for the scarcity of time and the fierce want to make every moment count.

Ultimately, urgency is this: Are you playing to win? Winning demands urgency. Without urgency... well, that's a slow road to irrelevance.

So, light a fire under your organization. Inject every meeting, every decision, every action with a sense of urgency. Your investors will thank you, and your competitors will fear you.

DESTINATION FIVE - EXECUTION

Beyond the Whiteboard, Executing on Strategic Vision

Welcome to execution, where grand plans become glorious realities or fade into the graveyard of good intentions. If you're expecting a dull lecture on project management, you're in for a surprise. This is where we separate the doers from the dreamers, the achievers from the excuse-makers.

Every action a company takes must serve its goal. Whether your strategy is profit-driven or philanthropic, flawless execution is the only path to success. Each decision, each initiative, and each employee's effort must align with this singular purpose. There's no room for wasted motion or misaligned priorities. Your strategy sets the destination, but it's relentless, focused execution that will get you there. Without it, even the most brilliant plans are nothing more than wishful thinking.

In my years in leadership roles, I've learned lessons: a mediocre strategy executed brilliantly often outperforms a brilliant strategy executed poorly.

Execution isn't sexy. It doesn't get the glamorous headlines or the standing ovations at shareholder meetings. It's the grunt work, the daily grind, the thousand little decisions and actions that add up to success or failure. It's also where most companies falter.

Why? Because execution is complex. It requires discipline, attention to detail, and aligning your organization towards common goals. Execution demands that you, as a leader, roll up your sleeves and get your hands dirty. It's not barking orders from an ivory tower; it's being in the trenches with your team, clearing obstacles, and making things happen.

EXECUTION AS A CONTINUOUS PROCESS

The Infinite Journey

Execution is not a finite task but a continuous journey, turning intent into operational reality, a perpetual cycle of planning, action, learning, and adaptation.

Project completion doesn't end the execution journey, nor does achieving a goal. Each milestone is merely a waypoint in the broader journey. Successful organizations maintain momentum, reassessing the landscape and adjusting course as needed.

This continuous approach to execution requires a mindset shift, moving you away from the idea of strategy as a fixed plan to follow and towards a more dynamic, adaptive view. Recognizing that the ability to execute is a business advantage that sets an organization apart in a competitive landscape.

Continuous execution requires leaders and teams to stay attuned to market changes, shifts in customer needs, and emerging opportunities or threats. It also means being willing to challenge assumptions, even those that underpin current strategies.

This approach emphasizes learning. Each execution generates further comprehension about the market, the organization's capabilities, and what works and what doesn't. Capturing and applying these lessons is imperative for refining future execution efforts and informing strategic thinking.

Technology plays an important role in continuous execution. Data analytics, AI, and other tools offer real-time performance insights, helping organizations spot trends, find issues, and make informed decisions. But these tools enhance human judgment; they don't replace it. Leadership in this context creates an environment where adaptability, encouraging calculated risk-taking, building resilience, and continuous execution thrive. Leaders must balance the need for consistent direction with the flexibility to pivot when circumstances demand it.

Viewing execution as continuous helps to bridge the often-cited gap between strategy and implementation. It acknowledges that strategy and execution are inseparable, working together rather than as separate activities.. The insights gained through execution inform and refine strategy, creating a virtuous cycle of learning and improvement.

The ability to execute and adapt swiftly becomes indispensable. Those who master this art of continuous execution are better positioned to survive and thrive, turning the challenges of a dynamic environment into opportunities for growth and innovation.

Execution is an organizational ability. It is a system that consistently translates intent into real-world results, adapts to changing circumstances, and drives continuous improvement. By embracing execution as a constant process, organizations build the agility, resilience, and focus to turn their boldest strategies into enduring success.

A Systems Thinking Approach

The Art and Science of Execution

Before we dive into the nitty-gritty of execution, let's talk systems. In a business, everything's connected, a giant web of cause and effect. Systems thinking lets you see these connections. It's understanding that tweaking one aspect of your business causes ripples (or tsunamis) elsewhere. It's holistic, interconnected, and the key to navigating the complexity of modern business.

The goal of every for-profit business is the same. Use resources (money, people, materials, intellectual property, and institutional knowledge) to create value.

To reach these goals, you need a system that creates an output.

> "A bad system will beat a good person every time."–William Edwards Deming.

Companies often find themselves caught in a whirlwind of challenges. Endless hurdles, from streamlining operations to improving product development, enhancing customer service, and optimizing resources. Organizations fall into the trap of addressing these issues in isolation, applying band-aid solutions that give temporary relief but cannot solve underlying systemic problems.

What is a system?

A "system" is not a haphazard collection of things. It's like a finely tuned engine, where each part, from the spark plugs to the pistons, works in concert to generate power and propel the vehicle forward.

It's an interconnected network of elements, think people, processes, resources, and even collaborative ideas that achieve a shared goal. It's the individual parts and how they interact, influence one another, and create something more than the sum of their parts. Consider a bustling city, a thriving ecosystem, or even the intricate workings of the human brain. These are complex systems where the whole is far more than a collection of its constituent parts.

However, here's the intriguing part: systems are dynamic, ever-evolving, and often unpredictable. They respond to feedback, adapt to their surroundings, and show emergent behaviors that catch us off guard. It's akin to navigating a sailboat through a storm. You chart a course, but be prepared to adjust your sails as the winds change.

Understanding a system requires taking a step back, observing the bigger picture, and identifying subtle connections, feedback loops, and patterns that shape its behavior.

What Drives System Output?

A system has inputs. They are resources, money, materials, intellectual property, and mission goals (do you remember the mission and aspirations statements?). The purpose of the system is to convert the inputs into value. Profit is when the cost of converting resources is less than the value created.

Continuous improvement aims to widen the gap between cost and value and increase conversion speed. The system is driven by people subjected to constraints. Those constraints are processes, rules, infrastructure, and tools. If we want to increase profit and move faster, we must improve the things contributing to cost, output, and speed.

They are:

Mission Processes and Rules

These are like the software development methodologies and project management frameworks of a technology business. They give the structure and guidelines for creating new products and features, ensuring timely delivery, and meeting quality standards. Your goal is to improve these processes to maximize the output and reduce the input needed to drive the processes.

People Processes and Rules

These are like a company's HR practices. They target attracting, developing, and keeping talented employees. Optimizing processes and rules benefits the organization by improving the productivity and quality of what the workforce delivers as input to the mission systems.

But hiring the right talent and optimizing processes is pointless if infrastructure and tools hamper the workforce. Landscapers don't use scissors to cut grass for a reason. They will get the job done, but the customer will find alternatives if the landscaper with scissors charges an hourly rate.

Infrastructure, Tools, and Resources

Infrastructure, tools, and resources are the backbone of any successful operation, providing the essential support and capabilities that help individuals and organizations achieve their goals. Whether it's the physical infrastructure of office facilities with its desk chairs or tools such as programming languages, cloud computing platforms, testing frameworks, and collaboration software, which developers build and deploy software with efficiently, or the resources like free coffee that gives the workforce that brief boost, the digital tools that streamline communication and collaboration, or the financial resources that fuel innovation and growth, these elements play a role in facilitating progress and productivity. By investing in robust infrastructure, adopting the right tools, and securing adequate resources, we empower ourselves to overcome challenges and seize opportunities.

Here's where the systems thinking magic happens: every project and strategy is a chance to learn and improve. It's like perfecting your grandma's secret recipe. It takes time, patience, and a willingness to embrace the occasional kitchen mishap.

By approaching strategy and project execution with a systems thinking mindset, you're evolving your entire organization. You're creating a more resilient, adaptive, and innovative business ecosystem.

That slight improvement will be the butterfly effect leading to your next big breakthrough. So, think big, act systemically, and watch your business soar to new heights!

THE NOSEDIVE

The Art and Science of Execution

In record time, we'd delivered four state-of-the-art simulation systems to the United States Air Force, and we felt good. Only 90 to go. I/ITSEC (The Inter service/Industry Training, Simulation, and Education Conference), the Super Bowl of simulation and training trade shows, was around the corner. What could go wrong?

Spoiler alert: Everything.

Our team, decked out in business casual attire, with the company logo proudly displayed on our matching polo shirts, strutted into the meeting room like we owned the place. A wall of stern faces met us, over a dozen Air Force program office bigwigs, looking as if they'd bitten into particularly sour lemons.

A stone-faced Air Force program manager waited until we sat down. Then, with the gentleness of a sledgehammer, he dropped the bomb.

"We're canceling the program."

Our CEO, usually a smooth talker, looked like he'd been slapped with a breakfast kipper. "Why?" he croaked out.

The program manager flicked a switch in response, and the wall-mounted screen flickered to life. There it was, in its Excel spreadsheet glory, a defect log as endless as a tax code. Some were as severe as a paper cut, others... not so much.

"We've lost confidence in your ability to deliver," the program manager said, each word another nail in our corporate coffin.

I'd love to say we had a brilliant retort, a masterful presentation that turned it around. But we didn't. We were unprepared, like a sunbather in Glasgow in February. Somehow, through desperation, charm, and divine intervention, we convinced them to give us two weeks. Two weeks to pull a rabbit out of our hat, to turn water into wine, to... well, you get the idea.

As we shuffled out of that room, shell-shocked and reeling, one thought kept bouncing around my head: "How the hell are we going to fix this?"

Little did I know, our two-week countdown to redemption would become the corporate equivalent of a Mission Impossible movie, minus Tom Cruise and his stunts. But who needs stunts when saving a contract, right?

Stay tuned for the nail-biting conclusion, where we either pull off the business comeback of the century or spectacularly crash and burn. Either way, it's going to be one hell of a ride!

PRINCIPLES OF CRISIS MANAGEMENT

From Vision to Tangible Results

In the heat of a crisis, contingency plans go up in smoke.

"Bad companies are destroyed by crises; good companies survive them; great companies are improved by them."–Andy Grove, former CEO of Intel.

These moments forge true crisis management mettle, when leaders must navigate the chaos and rally their teams. The following principles aren't corporate buzzwords; they're the lifeblood of resilience in adversity.

Principle 1: Embrace the "Prepper" Mindset

As the tiger team had to expect every pitfall in their race against the clock, crisis managers must adopt a prepper mindset. They don't hope for the best; they plan for the worst.

This means war-gaming every conceivable scenario, building redundancies and fail-safes into systems, and establishing protocols for when things inevitably go sideways. Creating a state of readiness where everyone knows their role and is poised to leap into action at a moment's notice.

But as I learned, even the best-laid plans crumble under the weight of reality. That's why true preppers cultivate a mindset of adaptability, ready to pivot when the script goes out the window.

Principle 2: Decisiveness Beats Dithering

In a crisis, analysis paralysis is deadly. While leaders often fall victim to the "deer in headlights" syndrome, the moments they shine brightest are when they act with swift decisiveness.

When the Air Force dropped the cancellation bombshell, the team didn't waste precious time wringing their hands. We began mounting a last-ditch, fourteen-day offensive to save the contract.

Decisive crisis managers understand that imperfect action beats perfect inaction every time. They empower frontline responders to make judgment calls at the moment, understanding that a flawed decision is often better than no decision. Dithering and delay are luxuries they can't afford.

Principle 3: Transparency Trumps "Spin"

The disaster at the I/ITSEC trade show illustrates the perils of spinning your way out of a crisis. When major defects surfaced, the instinct was to downplay and deflect, hoping the problems will solve themselves.

But as is often said, "sunlight is the best disinfectant." Savvy crisis managers understand that attempts at obfuscation or sugar-coating backfire in the era of radical transparency. The cover-up becomes worse than the crime.

Instead, they default to openness and honesty, even when the facts are uncomfortable. They know that trust is the most precious currency in a crisis and that unflinching transparency is the fastest way to rebuild confidence.

Principle 4: Agility is the Antidote to Uncertainty

If the story teaches us anything, no plan survives first contact with the enemy.

In the fog of crisis, the only certainty is uncertainty. Rigid, overly prescriptive plans become anchors, drowning organizations in irrelevance. The antidote is agility - the ability to adapt to changing circumstances.

This means building flexibility in decision-making frameworks, empowering teams to course-correct on the fly, embracing improvisation, and recognizing that the "perfect" approach is often the enemy of the 'good enough' solution in a fast-moving crisis.

Principle 5: Resilience is a Team Sport

Perhaps the most inspiring lesson is the power of a unified, tenacious team in adversity. When the contract cancellation hit, it would have been easy for the team to splinter and point fingers. Instead, they banded together, drawing strength from a shared purpose.

Crisis management recognizes that resilience is a team sport. No single hero can shoulder the burden alone. It takes a collective effort, with everyone playing their part with grit and determination.

Fostering a resilient, 'all-for-one' staff is the ultimate task of crisis leadership. It means leading by example, celebrating minor victories, and having the team's back during tough times. Because when a team believes in overcoming together, they do.

From Principles to Practice

Mastering these crisis management principles is one thing - putting them into practice is another. It takes more than a clever catchphrase to navigate the storm. It takes sweat, improvisation, and sheer force of will. But for those willing to embrace the prepper mindset, act with decisive courage, lead with transparency, adapt with agility, and cultivate collective resilience, even the most daunting crisis becomes a defining moment of triumph.

Ask the Tiger team. They didn't weather the storm; they emerged stronger, wiser, and more battle-tested than ever. And that's the true mark of crisis management excellence.

CHAOS AND A DESPERATE GAMBIT

The Quest to Save $110 Million

The day after our near-death experience with the Air Force, our illustrious management team gathered for what I describe as the corporate equivalent of a dumpster fire.

Overseen by the CEO, there we were, a collection of vice presidents, supposedly the cream of the company crop, a sprinkling of department directors, plus me, a lowly product manager. I say "team" loosely because what unfolded was as cohesive as a herd of cats on roller skates.

I watched these industry titans engage in high-stakes bickering for two excruciating hours. It was like watching a reality TV show where the prize was our company's survival, and everyone competed to be the biggest diva. There was more posturing than a bodybuilding competition and as much progress as a sloth on tranquilizers.

Our fearless leaders had a long and illustrious history of management by committee, a fancy term for let's talk in circles until we forget why we're here. By the end of this farce, we were no closer to a solution than we were to colonizing Mars.

As I left that room, I felt a cocktail of emotions swirling in my gut, one part fury, two parts frustration, with a dash of why the hell did I move from the UK for this circus. I designed the solution, worked with our engineers, and played ringmaster in the customer demonstration. There was no way I would watch it go up in flames because our management team couldn't find their collective backside with both hands and a map.

That evening, as I navigated the streets of Montreal on my way home, something inside me snapped. In a moment of temporary insanity (or genius), I called our CEO, Lionel.

"Lionel," I said, throwing caution to the wind, "you were in that room. We can't solve this by committee. These guys were more concerned with impressing you than fixing the problem."

Lionel, bless him, agreed. Emboldened, I went for broke.

"Give me the authority," I said, heart pounding. "Let me direct the management team and lead this effort. I'll fix this mess."

There was a pause. I held my breath, wondering if I'd talked myself out of a job.

Then, without missing a beat, Lionel said, "Go for it. I'll make the announcement first thing in the morning."

In an instant, I'd gone from spectator to gladiator. The fate of our contract now rested squarely on my shoulders.

Did I pull off this Hail Mary pass? Well, that's a story that follows. But let me tell you, the next two weeks were going to make that management meeting look like a picnic in comparison. Get ready folks; this ride is getting bumpy!

The Day I Became Corporate Overlord

A Tale of a Conference Room Coup

As the Montreal sun peeked over the snow and ice-covered horizon, I sat in my office, plotting. I was a Bond villain, minus the white cat. The task ahead was Everest-sized, and I knew that diplomacy had no place in this rescue mission. No, this called for something more... let's call it "menacingly assertive leadership." Or, you know, a benevolent dictatorship.

Lionel had dropped the email bomb. The management team members were now officially my minions. I mean, "direct reports." Same difference, right?

I summoned them to my lair... er, office, one by one. Picture the scene: me channeling my inner Darth Vader (minus the heavy breathing), and them, looking as if they'd been called to the principal's office.

Did I approach this with fear and trepidation? Please. I was as nervous as a lion facing a herd of particularly dim-witted gazelles. I laid out their marching orders with the subtlety of a sledgehammer to the face. My expectations weren't clear; they were crystal, diamond, see-through-your-soul clear.

Now, you will think this new world order ruffled feathers. And boy, did it ever. A few brave (or foolish) souls offered 'alternatives' to my instructions. Bless their hearts. I shut them down faster than you saying "corporate restructuring." They pleaded with the CEO to have him change his mind. That man was not for turning. We had no time for arguments or discussions. This was triage, not a debate club.

By midday, the message had sunk; a new sheriff was in town, and I wasn't handing out gold stars for participation. The air was thick with resentment, fear, and, dare I say it, a smidgen of respect. Or was that the smell of burning egos? Hard to tell.

As I sat surveying my new kingdom, I couldn't help but wonder: Was this how William Wallace felt before facing the English? Let's hope my campaign ends better than his did.

This corporate rollercoaster was leaving the station. Next stop: either glorious victory or spectacular, career-ending disaster. Care to place your bets?

THE RESCUE MISSION

All or Nothing

With the weight of the company's most important contract on my shoulders and a ticking clock, I knew that our salvation lay not in my abilities but in the collective genius of our team. It was time to rally the troops and leverage every ounce of talent our company offered.

First order of business: tearing apart the silos. I called an all-hands meeting, bringing together every department, from engineering to customer services, from program managers and purchasing to the finance wizards. The message was simple: we were one team with one mission for the next two weeks.

"Listen up," I began, my voice carrying across the packed conference room. "We've got two weeks to save this contract, and I need every single one of you. Forget your job titles. Forget your usual responsibilities. We will approach this problem from every angle, using every skill set we have."

I saw the mix of fear and excitement in their eyes. Good. We needed that energy.

Next, I set up a war room. We soon covered the walls with whiteboards, sticky notes, and diagrams. It resembled a conspiracy theorist's dream, but was our roadmap to redemption.

I assigned cross-functional teams, deliberately mixing people who rarely worked together. "I want fresh perspectives," I said. "Challenge each other. Question everything."

Our software engineers huddled with the subject-matter experts, brainstorming ways to visualize our progress. Financial analysts worked alongside project managers, crunching numbers and timelines. Even the marketing team got involved, helping to craft our message to the Air Force.

I encouraged wild ideas, no matter how outlandish. "There are no bad ideas, only unexplored opportunities," I repeated like a mantra.

As the hours ticked by, I moved from group to group, listening, challenging, and encouraging. I saw our customer services rep strike up a conversation with a senior developer. Their discussion sparked an idea that became a part of our proposal.

We worked around the clock, fueled by caffeine, determination, and the genuine fear of failure. But amidst the chaos, something beautiful was happening. Barriers were breaking down, and innovations were emerging from unexpected places.

By the end of the first week, we had the bones of a plan. It wasn't perfect, but it was bold. It addressed the immediate issues and showed a fundamental shift in how we approached project management and client relationships.

As we refined our proposal, I ensured every team member understood their role in its creation. This wasn't my plan or the management team's plan. It belonged to everyone.

The night before our presentation to the Air Force, I gathered the team one last time. They were exhausted, but their fierce pride in our accomplishments was clear.

"Tomorrow, when we walk into that room, we're presenting a plan. We're showing the Air Force who we are as a company. We show them our commitment, innovation, and ability to come together in adversity,." I said.

Looking around at the nodding heads and determined expressions, I knew we were ready. Win or lose, we had achieved something remarkable. We had transformed from a collection of departments into a unified force capable of taking on any challenge.

The following day, as we marched into the Air Force briefing room, I felt the strength of every team member behind me. We weren't only fighting for a contract. We were fighting for each other, for the work we'd poured our hearts into.

I took a deep breath and began our presentation, ready to show the Air Force brass a plan and the power of a unified team.

FROM THE BRINK OF DISASTER TO TRIUMPH

Crisis Management and Execution

We had convinced the Air Force to trust us and not to cancel the contract. We had to execute, and we did.

Our issues stemmed from more than technical glitches. Communication breakdowns, misaligned priorities, and inefficient workflows contributed to our problems.

We showed the Air Force a fundamental shift in how we operated.

"This is impressive," the Air Force program manager admitted after witnessing an extensive simulator test. A ghost of a smile playing on his lips. "But can you deliver the remaining 90 systems in 48 months?"

"We will do better than that," I replied, feeling a surge of confidence. "With this approach, we will speed up the remaining deliveries from four years to under two."

There was a moment of stunned silence, followed by a flurry of questions. We spent the next hour detailing our longer-term logistics plans, showing how our approach solved the current issues and improved efficiency and quality.

By the end of the test and review phase, we saved the contract and secured an agreement for the sped-up delivery schedule. As we shook hands with the Air Force team, I saw the respect in their eyes. We weren't contractors anymore; we were partners.

The journey that followed was intense but incredibly rewarding. True to our word, we delivered 90 additional simulation systems in under two years. They exceeded expectations in ways we hadn't even expected. The simulator has become the most prolific product in its category, easily outselling the combined sales of our competitors.

That crisis was the best thing that could have happened to us. It forced us to reevaluate everything, challenge our assumptions, and embrace a more holistic, systems-based approach. Saving the contract transformed our entire company.

The product revolutionized their training capabilities. We discovered that our greatest strength wasn't in our technology but in our ability to adapt, think systematically, and never give up.

The $110 million nosedive had become the most remarkable ascent of our company's history.

Lessons from the Brink

What My Story Can Teach Us About Execution Excellence

The story is a class in execution under extreme duress. From the heady rush of landing a game-changing contract to the gut-wrenching realization that it was going to slip away, our journey illuminates both the perils and the promises of high-stakes execution. As we've seen, success in these make-or-break moments requires a delicate alchemy of leadership, teamwork, and sheer force of will.

The Power of 'Benevolent Dictatorship.'

When crisis struck, I didn't have the luxury of consensus-building or gentle persuasion. With the clock ticking and millions on the line, I had to assert control swiftly and decisively. The "benevolent dictatorship" approach, setting crystal-clear expectations and brooking no dissent, was necessary for crisis leadership.

This doesn't suggest that autocracy is the answer to every execution challenge. But in moments of existential peril, leaders must take command, make tough calls, and steer the ship with an iron hand. Hesitation and equivocation are luxuries they can't afford.

Breaking Down Silos, Building Up Collective Genius

Faced with a challenging task, I knew our salvation lay in the team's collective genius. The first move was to tear down the walls between departments, forcing cross-functional collaboration at every turn.

By mixing unlikely combinations, we unlocked fresh perspectives and sparked innovation. The war room became a crucible of creativity. We welcomed wild ideas and challenged conventional wisdom.

The lesson is clear: when the stakes are highest, silos are your enemy. Execution excellence demands breaking down barriers, a free flow of ideas, and harnessing every ounce of organizational talent. Only by bringing every voice to the table will breakthrough solutions emerge.

The Motivating Force of Ownership

As the team burned the midnight oil, fueled more by adrenaline than by caffeine, I ensured that every team member felt a sense of ownership over the plan they were crafting.

This wasn't management's or engineering's plan; It was ours. Collectively birthed through sweat, tears, and sheer determination. That sense of ownership became a powerful motivating force, driving the team to heights they never knew they could reach.

Too often, in the heat of execution, the "doers" become divorced from the "deciders." But true excellence demands a deep sense of ownership at every level. When team members have their fingerprints on the final product, they'll move mountains to make it succeed.

The Transformative Power of Adversity

The story's most profound lesson is adversity's transformative power. Faced with a crisis that could have easily torn us apart, the team found a new sense of unity and purpose.

The threat of failure became a galvanizing force, forging new bonds of trust and respect. In the crucible of that high-stakes environment, a collection of departments became a band of brothers and sisters, ready to stand shoulder-to-shoulder in the face of any challenge.

It's a reminder that our greatest triumphs often spring from our darkest moments. Faced with impossible odds reveals true character. And it's those trial-by-fire experiences that transform mere teams into unstoppable forces.

Execution Excellence: An Enduring Quest

The story carries universal truths about what it takes to achieve execution excellence. Bold leadership in crisis moments, harnessing collective genius, instilling a deep sense of ownership, and finding opportunity and unity in adversity.

But above all, it's a reminder that execution excellence is an enduring quest, not a onetime achievement. It demands a willingness to learn from missteps and a readiness to adapt.

The teams that embrace this and see every crisis as an opportunity and every challenge as a chance to get better are the ones that thrive. They're the ones who emerge from the crucible stronger, wiser, and more capable than they ever dreamed possible. And they're the ones that light the way for those who aspire to turn visions into reality.

A Legacy of Learning and Continuous Improvement

Teaching the Next Batch

In the control tower of New York's John F. Kennedy International Airport, Michael, a veteran air traffic controller, gazed out at the sprawling runways, his eyes tracking the movements of countless planes with practiced ease. As he guided a Boeing 787 to its gate, his mind drifted to his upcoming lecture to a group of recruits. The topic: "Discipline and Continuous Improvement in Air Traffic Management."

Michael had been in the industry for over three decades, and he knew that the safety of millions of passengers rested on the shoulders of professionals like him. Their skills kept the skies safe but needed the industry's unwavering commitment to learning from the past and striving for improvement to complete the picture.

As his shift ended and he went to the training center, Michael reflected on the key examples he wanted to share with the eager, youthful faces he would soon meet. Etched into his memory as tragic events and pivotal moments, each story reshaped the industry to which he had dedicated his life.

Michael recounted the story of United Airlines Flight 232 in 1989. "A catastrophic engine failure led to the loss of the hydraulic systems," he said. "Crash-landing the plane with survivors was miraculous."

He described how this incident improved maintenance procedures and enhanced pilot training for managing total hydraulic failure scenarios. "In our job," he emphasized, "we must be prepared for the impossible. Every scenario we train for, every procedure we follow, is built on lessons learned from incidents like Flight 232."

Michael then turned to the 2009 Air France Flight 447 disaster, a flight from Brazil to France. Inconsistent airspeed indications and miscommunication led to the pilots inadvertently stalling the plane. They didn't recover from the stall, and the plane crashed into the mid-Atlantic, killing the 228 passengers and crew on board. "This incident highlighted the interplay between human operators and advanced technology," he explained. He described how the crash improved pilots' training in handling high-altitude stalls and unreliable airspeed indications.

"As air traffic controllers, we work with innovative technology daily," Michael said. "But we never forget that our judgment, our ability to interpret and act on information, is our most valuable tool. Continuous training and improving our skills are not optional. It's a fundamental part of our job."

Finally, Michael addressed the disappearance of Malaysia Airlines Flight 370 (MH370) in 2014. MH370, a passenger flight, disappeared en-route from Kuala Lumpur to Beijing. Shortly after departing, the aircraft veered off course and lost contact with air traffic control. Despite extensive international search efforts, search teams only found some debris in the Indian Ocean, leaving the precise cause of the disaster and the location of MH370 unknown. "This ongoing mystery pushed our industry to examine how it is possible to lose track of an entire plane in the 21st century."

He explained how this incident led to new global flight-tracking systems. "Every flight you track, every handoff you make to the next sector," he told the recruits, "is part of a global system designed to make sure no plane ever disappears again."

As Michael concluded his lecture, he looked at the recruits' faces, seeing a mix of solemnity and determination. "These tragedies, as heartbreaking as they are, have made our skies safer. They are stark reminders of the need for discipline in our daily operations and continuous improvement in our systems and procedures."

He paused, letting the weight of his words sink in. "Air traffic management isn't only a job," he continued. "It's a commitment to learning, improving, and never becoming complacent. You're not only guiding planes when you step into that control room. You're carrying forward a legacy built on hard-learned lessons, prioritizing safety above everything else."

As the recruits filed out of the room, Michael knew that a more profound understanding of their responsibility had replaced a little of the eagerness. He smiled, knowing that the mindset of discipline and continuous improvement lived in this new generation of air traffic controllers.

DESTINATION SIX - DISCIPLINE

Secret Ingredient of Sustained Success

In the heat of execution, it's easy to become consumed by the immediate challenge. The adrenaline rush of a looming deadline and the thrill of rallying a team to achieve the impossible are the moments that capture our imagination and fuel our drive. But even the most heroic feats of execution are fleeting victories if not underpinned by something more enduring: discipline.

Discipline is the unglamorous but essential counterpart to execution brilliance. It's the daily commitment to continuous improvement, the relentless pursuit of better processes, smoother workflows, and more elegant solutions. If execution is the sprint, discipline is the marathon. This sustained, systematic effort turns isolated wins into long-term success.

At the heart of this discipline lies a deceptively simple tool: measurement. The phrase "you can't manage what you can't measure" is especially true in execution. Only by rigorously tracking process inputs and outputs are the bottlenecks that throttle productivity, the inefficiencies that waste precious resources, and the leverage points where targeted improvements yield outsized results identified.

This is where the combined power of systems thinking and the theory of constraints come into play. We pinpoint the critical constraints that limit our overall performance by viewing our execution challenges through the lens of interconnected systems. Improvement efforts focus on where they'll have the most impact, continually optimizing and fine-tuning until we've squeezed every drop of potential from our processes.

Continuous Improvement

It Does What It Says on the Tin

Every near-miss is a wake-up call. As a business leader, MBA graduate, air traffic controller, and accidental strategist, I've found myself fascinated by the parallels between the intricate dance of planes orchestrated by the men and women in control towers and radar rooms and their application to value creation and leadership. Aviation offers a treasure trove of insights for any organization committed to continuous improvement and safety.

You are standing in a bustling air traffic control center. Screens flicker with countless blips, each representing lives in transit. Controllers speak in clipped, precise tones, guiding metal birds through invisible lanes. In this environment, there's no room for error. Yet, errors occur. And when they do, the response is not one of panic or blame but of rigorous analysis and learning.

The air traffic control system's approach to incidents is a lesson in continuous improvement. Each event, whether a loss of separation between aircraft or a runway incursion, is a golden opportunity to enhance safety measures. This mindset separates good organizations from great ones. You don't need perfection; you need relentless refinement and adaptation.

Consider the case of the 2002 Überlingen mid-air collision. Two planes collided over Germany because of a complex series of events and factors, including short-staffing in the control room and conflicting instructions between the controller and the aircraft's collision avoidance system. The investigation didn't simply point fingers at the controller on duty. Instead, it peeled back layers of systemic issues, leading to fundamental changes in air traffic control procedures across Europe and beyond.

The lesson here extends beyond aviation. In any business, finding a scapegoat is simple when something goes wrong. The infinitely more valuable approach is to ask: What have we learned from this? How do we improve our systems to prevent similar incidents in the future?

Air traffic control also highlights the critical role of technology in driving improvement. Advanced conflict detection software, digital flight progress strips, and sophisticated simulators for training emerged from a commitment to continuous enhancement. In our businesses, are we leveraging technology effectively? Are we seeking new tools and methods to improve our operations?

Organizations must strive for the air traffic control community's open reporting practices. The air traffic control community encourages controllers to report errors, near-misses, and potential safety issues without fear of punitive action. This creates a rich data set and helps identify potential problems before they lead to accidents. Imagine the potential for improvement if every employee in your organization felt empowered to speak up about inefficiencies or safety concerns.

But perhaps the most profound lesson to learn from air traffic control is the effectiveness of collaborative improvement. The global nature of air travel causes international cooperation in developing and implementing safety enhancements. Look beyond the walls of your business and engage in industry collaborations and knowledge sharing to drive collective improvement.

As business leaders, we must ask ourselves: Are we treating our close calls as learning opportunities? We're not talking about celebrating failure here. We are rewriting our collective mindset to see setbacks as the raw materials for our next leap forward. Are we ready to flip the script on how we view mistakes, transforming them from cringe-worthy moments into catalysts for growth? Are we leveraging data and technology to enhance our decision-making processes?

The path of continuous improvement is difficult. But as the air traffic control community has shown us, it's a path leading to safer skies and, in the business world, more resilient, innovative, and successful organizations.

So the next time your business faces a setback, channel the spirit of air traffic control. Approach the problem with the same level of focus and precision. Dig deep to understand the root causes. Use data to drive your decisions. Encourage open reporting. View every near-miss not as a close shave but as an opportunity to fine-tune your systems and soar to greater heights.

Like those invisible highways in the sky, the path to excellence is about developing the systems and mindset to navigate safely, learning, and improving with every mile.

The Discipline of Continuous Improvement

Whether in the bustling control room of an air traffic management center or the boardroom of a Fortune 500 company, success is a double-edged sword. While it brings rewards and recognition, it also carries an insidious danger: complacency. This silent threat lurks in the shadows of achievement, waiting for lowered guards and waning vigilance.

The annals of history are rife with tales of triumph turned to tragedy, of market leaders toppled from their pedestals because they fell victim to the lull of complacency. It's a cruel irony that the signs of impending disaster often manifest themselves when it's too late to avert the course. Like a cancer that grows undetected until it reaches a critical stage, organizational decay occurs long before its symptoms become apparent.

The controller doesn't glance at an aircraft's position once and assumes its trajectory will remain constant. They don't check a flight's altitude and then forget about it for the next several minutes. Instead, their eyes sweep their assigned sector, absorbing and processing information in a practiced pattern. Position, altitude, speed, and heading checking and rechecking for each aircraft are ongoing. With each scan, the controller asks, "What do I do if...?" What if that aircraft suddenly deviates from its course?

Companies adopting a 'continuous improvement' process must approach it with the same discipline and consistency. It's not enough to implement improvements and then sit back, basking in the glow of a job well done. Actual continuous improvement is ongoing and relentless.

Success is a constant change, refinement, and improvement. When an organization believes it has "arrived" and can afford to relax its guard, it becomes vulnerable to disruption or disaster.

The mindset of continuous improvement is the responsibility of everyone in the organization. We have discussed the contributions of **Re**search, **E**valuation, **S**trategy, **C**ommunications, and **E**xecution to the aim of value creation. Let's look at **D**iscipline and the driver of everything we do: processes.

A CEO's Awakening

The Board's Fixation with Lagging Indicators

Every month, there was a board meeting; overkill, but I had to comply. I spent hours collating and formatting board reports.

Most board meeting time was used to discuss financial metrics and forecasts. With hindsight, this was a mistake. Our world was closely linked to government budget cycles. Government customers start procurement as often as two or three years before the expected budget approval. Sometimes, that approval never came; there were other priorities. Revenue forecasting was, at best, a guessing game. Frustratingly, much of the revenue came from contracts that never appeared in the extended forecasts. More worryingly were the margin and cost metrics. What was the reason for the fall or climb in project gross margins? What caused the change in overhead costs that impacted EBITDA? With a brief investigation, we had some answers for the next board meeting; by then, everything had changed again. It was a frustrating process.

The question here is, how do financial metrics help the company's operations? When the bad news hits, there is often little you can do about it. Any correctional initiatives you make can take months to impact the business.

Don't get me wrong, financial metrics are important as a report card of business (and leadership) performance. But financial metrics are lagging indicators. Surely detecting problems before they affect financial performance is what we need?

I needed more. I needed metrics to help us predict future outcomes, 'leading indicators.'

Leading Indicators

An Organizations Crystal Ball

Knowing what to measure is part science, part art. It espouses understanding your business's rhythm, processes' flow, and market pulse. So, channel your inner detective, and start investigating. Your business's hidden insights are waiting to be discovered!

Leading indicators serve as the canaries in the coal mine, offering early warnings of potential disruptions or safety concerns. These proactive measures allow controllers, pilots, and management to expect challenges and adapt strategies before issues manifest as serious incidents.

In the headquarters of a global automotive parts manufacturer, a team of analysts huddled around a series of dashboards but not glued to the usual quarterly production figures and sales numbers. Instead, they focused on metrics that, at first glance, seem disconnected from the core business. They were the company's leading indicators, early warning signals designed to illuminate potential problems long before they appeared in the factory or on the balance sheet.

One screen, monitored by a supply chain expert, displayed supplier delivery times. Over the past three months, a subtle but consistent increase had caught their attention. The supply chain expert noticed a trend: potential parts shortages, stalled production lines, and, ultimately, unhappy customers.

Nearby, a quality assurance team member scrutinized employee training hours across departments. A recent dip in training time for quality control staff correlated with an uptick in product defect rates. Though not statistically significant, the connection raised a red flag for those attuned to such patterns.

Across the room, a market research specialist observed a dashboard displaying social media sentiment around electric vehicles and autonomous driving technology. The data revealed a growing buzz among their target demographic, hinting at a potential market shift reshaping the entire automotive landscape.

These disparate leading indicators depicted potential challenges and opportunities looming. The lengthening supplier delivery times whispered of possible supply chain disruptions. The dip in training hours hinted at future quality control issues. The social media chatter pointed to evolving consumer desires and future product development.

Armed with these early warning signs, the company can take proactive steps. The procurement team diversifies its supplier base to mitigate potential shortages. Human resources invest in targeted training programs to uphold quality standards. The product development team speeds up research and development efforts in emerging technologies to stay ahead.

This proactive, data-driven approach, guided by selected leading indicators, empowers the company to navigate the complexities of the market with agility and foresight. Rather than reacting to crises, they expect and address potential issues before they impact the financial outcome.

The following sections will explore how businesses across industries can harness leading indicators. We'll discuss selecting the right metrics for your needs, accurately interpreting their signals, and translating those insights into action, using the 4Ms method: map the system and processes, measure the process outputs, monitor the process outputs, modify the processes

Rinse and repeat.

From predicting market shifts to forecasting operational bottlenecks, leading indicators offer a potent tool for any organization seeking to thrive in an unpredictable business environment.

MAPPING

Mapping the System and Processes, The First M

The first M, mapping, takes us back to systems thinking. Mapping your business systems will be daunting, particularly in large companies. Do not skip this process; the return on investment will be worth it. Mapping is your 'Big Picture.' It is the enabler of three-dimensional thinking.

Systems and process mapping is a fundamental tool in the arsenal of any business professional seeking to understand, analyze, and improve organizational operations. Process mapping is the visual representation of activities that transform inputs into outputs, creating a roadmap of how work gets done within an organization. This powerful technique allows managers and teams to gain a bird's-eye view of complex workflows, identifying bottlenecks, redundancies, and opportunities for enhancement that otherwise remain hidden in the day-to-day bustle of business operations. By breaking down processes into their constituent steps and illustrating the flow of information and materials, process mapping provides a common language for discussing and refining organizational procedures. Whether applied to a manufacturing production line, a customer service workflow, or a complex decision-making process, this visual approach to process analysis catalyzes continuous improvement, fostering clarity, efficiency, and innovation across every level of an organization.

If this is your first mapping exercise, a good place to start is identifying the company's revenue-generation steps, i.e., things the organization does that relate to finding prospects and turning them into customers.

For this example, we will use the customer journey or, more specifically, the steps taken to find the prospects and move them through the process of becoming a customer. The customer journey refers to a customer's complete experience with a company or brand, starting from their first awareness of the brand or product and continuing through the purchase and post-purchase stages. Take this somewhat simplified version.

1. Find Prospective Customers

2. Lead Nurturing and Engagement

3. Convert Prospects into Customers

4. Deliver Products and Services

5. Collect Payment

6. Provide Support/Warranty

7. Customer Feedback

8. Customer Retention

9. Go Back to Step One

This list is an example. Your business will differ in its approach.

If you have difficulty deciding where to map your system, take inspiration from the company org chart. Look at the manager's roles and ask yourself what these departments' goals are. However, combining some responsibilities, such as sales and marketing, into a single department on the org chart is common. It is more useful to separate them for mapping and measuring purposes.

Once you have identified the customer journey as a series of steps, use the **Purpose**, **Method**, **Process**, **Who**, and **Dependency** questions to provide actionable information.

Purpose - What is the purpose of this step? It must be measurable, e.g., measure converting leads to customers by tracking the conversion percentage.

Method - How do we meet the purpose? There are several methods listed for each step in the map. For example, two methods identify prospective customers: inbound and outbound marketing, each driven by different processes. Methods describe the approach to satisfying the purpose.

Process- How we drive the method. What specific processes are being used? Inbound and outbound marketing has the same goal (identifying prospective customers) but takes different approaches to reaching them.

Who- What department or person is accountable for the step?

Dependency - What inputs are required to complete the processes, and who or what step depends on the output? Commonly, this will be the previous step and the next step on the map, but not always. A step can depend on multiple inputs. For example, software developers do not write code without software design documents; functional specifications lead to design documents; contract requirements, roadmaps, etc., drive functional specifications.

Steps	Purpose	Method	Processes	Who?	Dependency
Step 1 - Identify Prospective Customers	Identify potential customers (Leads)	Inbound and outbound marketing techniques	Content marketing, social media, SEO, email, etc.	Marketing Department	None
Step 2 - Lead Nurturing and Engagement	Move Prospects through the sales funnel	Direct engagement campaigns	Personalized emails, content marketing, webinars	Marketing and Sales Departments	Leads (Step 1)
Step 3 - Convert Prospects into Customers	Turn prospects into paying customers	Build a relationship in person or through communications	Sales scripts, product demos, free trials, special offers	Sales Department	Leads (Step 2)
Step 4 - Deliver Products and Services	Fulfill customer orders accurately and promptly	Digital products, hardware, services, etc.	Supply chain management, logistics, software development	Operations and Logistics Departments	Contracts, project management, product management
Step 5 - Collect Payment	Ensure timely and accurate payment collection	Accounting practices	Invoicing systems, payment methods, online payment gateways	Finance Department	Program management, contracts
Step 6 - Provide Support /Warranty	Improve customer retention and company reputation	Address customer issues and maintain satisfaction	Customer support, warranties, returns, maintenance services	Customer Support and Service Departments	Project/program management, contracts
Step 7 - Feedback and Continuous Improvement	Customer retention and new sales	Data collection and feedback	Conduct surveys, collect reviews, feedback sessions	Customer Success, Product Development, and QA Departments	Account management, ERP system, contracts
Step 8 - Customer Retention	Keep customers and encourage repeat business	Frequent communication and relationship building	Loyalty programs, discounts, exclusive content,	Marketing, Customer Success, Sales Departments	Sales, project management, customer support
Step 9 - Go Back to Step 1	Identify new prospects and expand the customer base	Use lessons learned and continuous improvement	Refine and optimize marketing strategies based on insights	Marketing, Customer Success, Sales Departments	Insights from customer journey and market research

Process Mapping Table

MEASURE

Knowing What to Measure, The Second M

In business processes, measuring everything is like boiling the ocean; It overwhelms, is impossible, and is unproductive. The key is knowing where to focus your efforts. Let's discuss how to do that without drowning in data.

Remember that system map we created? It's time to dust it off. Think of it as your treasure map, with each 'X' marking a potential insights goldmine. Each step in that example is a potential friction point. A bottleneck. These are parts of the system that give us leading indicators. But we won't dig at every 'X' we see. We're smarter than that.

Let's break down Purpose, Method, Process, Who, and Dependency.:

1. Purpose: What's the endgame here? It needs to be measurable. "Converting leads to customers" isn't corporate speak—it's a quantifiable goal.

2. Method: This is your game plan. We don't measure the method itself (that's like judging a book by its cover), but understanding it gives context to our measurements.

3. Process: This is where plans become action, and our measurements often come into play.

4. Who: Who's responsible for the process output? Knowing this helps with accountability and communication.

5. Dependency: What dominos need to fall before this process kicks into gear? This is the process input. Understanding these connections helps spot potential bottlenecks.

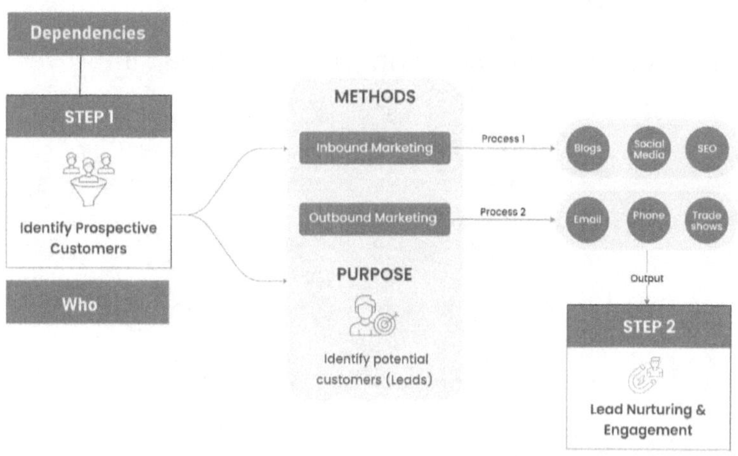

Step 1 - Dependency, Who, Method, Process

Your business has more processes than a restaurant has ingredients. Measuring them is a recipe for disaster (pun intended). So, how do we find that 'right' amount of measurement?

Let's take inbound marketing as our guinea pig. It's a beast with many heads. But do we need to slap a metric on every single sub-process? No.

Remember the first step in our inbound marketing journey? Goal setting. Ask yourself: What's the crown jewel of your campaign? Is it website traffic? Lead generation? Both? Whatever it is, that's where you plant your measurement flag.

"But wait! Isn't website traffic a lagging indicator?"

Think about it: Web visitors drive prospect identification. Prospects fuel conversions. It's a domino effect where each piece influences the next. A dip in web visits today means a prospect drought next month and a conversion famine the month after.

You might feel tempted to throw your hands up and say, "Why bother measuring inbound marketing? Let's count the prospects for the month and call it a day!"

Measuring the result (number of prospects) is valuable data, not the entire story. Knowing which approach (inbound or outbound marketing, for instance) is your star performer helps you decide where to double down or roll up your sleeves and improve.

How to Measure?

The Power of Process Behavior Charts

Imagine having a crystal ball that tells you when your business processes are improving or experiencing normal fluctuations. Well, process behavior charts are the next best thing. What are process behavior charts, and why are they a game-changer for businesses striving for continuous improvement?

Process behavior charts, also known as control charts or Shewhart charts, are statistical tools used to study how a process changes. These charts plot points against time.

Process behavior charts operate on a simple yet powerful principle: they help distinguish between common cause variation (natural fluctuations, 'noise,' in the process) and unique cause variation (unusual events or changes that require investigation).

1. Process behavior charts prevent the common mistake of reacting to every up and down in your data. They help you understand when a change is enough to warrant action, saving you from "tampering" with a stable process unnecessarily.

2. By visually representing your process over time, these charts help you spot trends or shifts before they become problematic. It's like having an early warning system for your processes.

3. Instead of chasing every data point, process behavior charts allow you to focus on systemic changes that lead to sustained improvement. They help you differentiate between one-off events and fundamental shifts in your process.

4. These charts provide a common language for discussing

process performance across an organization's levels. They make it easier to communicate complex statistical concepts to non-technical stakeholders.

5. By helping you understand the natural variation in your process, these charts allow you to predict future performance more accurately. This is invaluable for planning and resource allocation.

6. Detecting a unique cause variation starts an investigation into the root causes. This targeted approach to problem-solving leads to resilient and transformative solutions.

7. Process behavior charts provide a clear, statistical basis for determining whether changes to a process have resulted in genuine improvement. No more guessing or relying on gut feelings!

8. These charts result in cost savings in process management and improvement initiatives by reducing unnecessary interventions and focusing efforts where needed.

Process Behavior Charts - Putting It Together

This is not a book about process behavior charts, but to stimulate your interest, look at a couple of simple examples.

You're running a customer service department. Your process behavior chart tracks average call handling times. Over months (or whatever period is most appropriate for your process), you notice most points fall within the upper and lower control limits* - that's your process behaving normally.

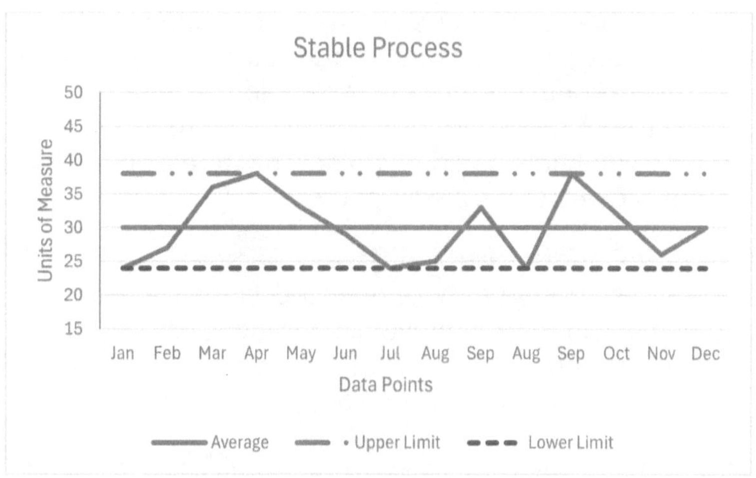

- Note -upper and lower limits are calculated from the data.

But then you spot from February to March and then three consecutive points (March, April, and May), below the lower control limit. This pattern suggests something has changed in your process; perhaps new, complex issues are arising, or there is a need for training. Without the chart, you miss the trend until it becomes a noticeable problem.

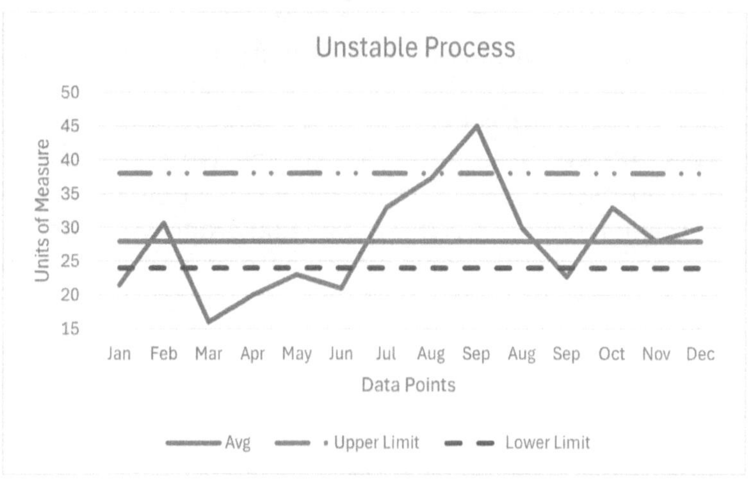

In August, you notice an obvious change in call handling times. This suggests something happened in the call-handling process. Was there a new product feature launch? Did you hire new call handlers with little or no experience? As you learn to use process behavior charts, you know one data point is not a reason to react. Investigate the cause, but it's a wait-and-see.

Process behavior charts are a different perspective on your processes. They encourage a more nuanced, statistical approach to understanding and improving your operations. By separating the signal from the noise, these charts empower you to make data-driven decisions that transform your business processes.

So, the next time you examine your business metrics, remember that a process behavior chart can be the tool you need to sharpen your continuous improvement efforts.

If this topic interests you, and it should, check out "Measures of Success" by Mark Graban.

In "Measures of Success," Mark Graban challenges the conventional wisdom of business metrics and performance management, offering an approach to understanding and improving processes. Drawing on the principles of process behavior charts, Graban shows how leaders distinguish between signal and noise in their data, avoiding the pitfalls of overreaction to normal variation while identifying authentic opportunities for improvement. With clarity and insight, he guides readers through the practical application of statistical methods that transform decision-making based on facts rather than gut feelings. "Measures of Success" is not only a book about charts and numbers; it's a paradigm shift in how we think about performance, promising to help organizations make better, more informed decisions that drive real, sustainable progress. Whether you're a seasoned executive or a front-line manager, Graban's work offers a roadmap to more proactive and visionary leadership through data-driven insight.

THE THEORY OF CONSTRAINTS

Finding Bottlenecks

The Theory of Constraints (TOC) is a management philosophy suggesting that one key factor or constraint limits every business. One bottleneck holds everything else back, like that one stubborn sheep that refuses to budge when you're herding the flock.

The idea is simple: identifying and fixing that constraint improves the entire system's performance. TOC isn't limited to factories or production lines. It's a universal concept applied to any business process, from customer service to marketing. It's as versatile as a good kilt, really.

Eliyahu M. Goldratt introduced TOC in his classic business novel *The Goal*, which tells the story of a manufacturing plant in crisis. Faced with inefficiencies, missed deadlines, and unhappy customers (a bit like the aftermath of a rowdy Hogmanay), the plant's management realizes they're focusing on the wrong things instead of fixing everything at once, a task as futile as draining a lake with a teaspoon, they zero in on the plant's biggest bottleneck, a machine that does not keep up with demand. They unlock improvements that transform the plant's fortunes by addressing that constraint.

While *The Goal* uses a manufacturing plant as its setting, the principles of TOC go far beyond the factory floor. Any business, whether a startup or a multinational corporation, can apply this approach. From a sales team struggling with follow-up processes to a software company bogged down by slow product development cycles, every organization has its version of a constraint. The trick is finding, prioritizing, and solving it.

TOC encourages a shift in mindset. Instead of scrambling to optimize everything immediately, focus on the one thing holding you back. Like the proverbial chain that's only as strong as its weakest link, a business only moves as fast as its biggest constraint. Address that, and you unlock performance improvements faster than a Scotsman chasing a rolling pound coin.

The TOC started and its principles apply to almost any business that wants to break through its limitations and reach extra levels of success. It's like finding the key to the whisky cabinet. Once you've got it, a world of possibilities opens up.

THE RUNWAY

A Practical Illustration of the Theory of Constraints

Imagine an air traffic control tower overseeing a busy international airport. Planes are on the runways, taxiways, and approach paths, everyone waiting for clearance to take off, land, or navigate the airspace. The airport's capacity is immense. Dozens of planes can land, take off, and taxi. Using one runway for take-offs and the other for landings improves efficiency. One small bottleneck throws the entire system into chaos.

Now, picture a scenario where the tower only has one runway while the other runway is undergoing maintenance. No matter how efficient the ground crews, the air traffic controllers, or the pilots are, the capacity of that single runway limits everything. It doesn't matter if the control tower manages the airspace perfectly or if the ground teams are lightning-fast at clearing planes off the runways. If that single runway gets overloaded, the entire system slows down. Planes circle the skies, waiting for clearance to land, and delays ripple across the airport.

This scenario perfectly illustrates the 'Theory of Constraints.' Here, the single operational runway is the constraint—the weakest link in the system. Improving the airport's efficiency is futile if they don't address the bottleneck. Even having the best pilots, advanced technology, and the most experienced controllers will not help. If the runway can't handle the volume of aircraft, the system will struggle.

Once the airport realizes the constraint is the runway, it can focus on solving that specific problem. This means prioritizing landing slots, improving runway clearance processes, or opening another runway as soon as possible. By focusing on the constraint, the airport reduces delays, improves safety, and gets the entire system running smoothly again.

Like this air traffic control example, every business has a 'runway' constraint that holds back its overall performance. The key is finding that bottleneck and then taking targeted actions to remove or reduce its impact. Systems and process mapping and measuring is your path to finding the problems. In managing the constraint, the complete business operates more efficiently, like a busy airport running at peak capacity after eliminating its runway bottleneck. But, like whack-a-mole, a new constraint often emerges after resolving the existing one. Keep whacking.

Modify

Process Improvement, The Third M

Systems thinking is your diagnostic tool. It's not finding and fixing a faulty part but understanding how the parts work together or don't. Start with your system and process maps. Not the idealized version gathering dust in your policy manual, the messy, coffee-stained reality of how work flows through your organization.

Get your team involved. They're the ones with grease under their fingernails. Ask them where they see bottlenecks, redundancies, or plain nonsense steps that make them want to headbutt their keyboards.

Prioritizing: Which Fire to Put Out First

Now, you've got a list of issues longer than the line at the DMV. How do you decide what to tackle first? Enter the Theory of Constraints.

Look for your system's constraint - the tightest bottleneck limiting overall performance. It's like finding the kink in a garden hose. Straighten that out, and suddenly, everything flows better.

Prioritize improvements that:

- Impact your constraint

- Have a ripple effect on multiple processes

- Are implemented quickly with minimal disruption

Remember, you're not aiming for perfection here. You're looking for progress. A twenty percent improvement in your primary constraint will do more for your bottom line than a one hundred percent improvement in a non-constrained area. Its like a funnel. It doesn't matter how much you can feed into the wide funnel opening, it matters how much can get through the narrow exit. Making the funnel opening wider has no effect.

Don't Trip Over Your Own Feet

Process improvement isn't a sprint. Here are some potholes to watch out for:

1. Don't get so caught up in mapping and measuring that you improve nothing. Perfect is the enemy of good enough.

2. The fanciest new process won't work if your team clings to old habits like a toddler on a security blanket. Change management isn't just buzzword bingo.

3. Dig deep. If customer complaints are rising, don't immediately hire more service reps. Find out why customers are complaining.

4. Processes are about people, not flowcharts. Engage your team, listen to their input, and remember that the most efficient process in the world is useless if your staff is miserable.

5. Implement, measure, adjust. Rinse and repeat. Continuous improvement is a way of life, not a break room poster.

Process improvement is about making your business a little less dysfunctional every day. Keep at it, and before you know it, you'll be cruising in that sports car, leaving your competitors in the dust.

Monitor

Monitoring Change, The Fourth M

After finding your constraint and implementing changes, it's tempting to consider the job done. However, monitoring the process outputs after these changes is consequential for preserving the reliability and performance of your business framework. This ongoing vigilance serves multiple vital purposes in the theory of constraints framework.

First, monitoring helps catch unintended consequences. Changes in one area of your system create ripple effects throughout. Systems maps and careful observation allow you to spot these effects before they escalate into troubling issues. While you have implemented a change with the best intentions, monitoring lets you confirm that your solution addresses the problem as intended.

The theory of constraints is 'continuous improvement.' An ongoing improvement process. As you address one bottleneck, another will inevitably emerge. Stick your finger in the hole in the dam and watch another leak sprout. Monitoring is your early warning system, helping you identify these new constraints. This perpetual cycle of identification and improvement is at the heart of TOC, and monitoring is the fuel that keeps this engine running.

Your business system is a complex network of interconnected processes, like a finely tuned machine. Regular maintenance ensures that parts are working in harmony, maintaining the overall integrity of your system. It provides you with concrete data and data-driven decision-making. Rather than relying on assumptions or gut feelings, you base your strategies and tactics on solid, measurable information.

This approach to monitoring and improvement also builds

stakeholder confidence. Showing concrete improvements or providing data-backed explanations for why an idea didn't work out stimulates and maintains support from internal and external stakeholders. It shows a commitment to transparency and continuous improvement that is invaluable in maintaining trust and securing resources for future initiatives.

In the world of business improvement, what gets measured gets managed. By keeping your metrics sharp and monitoring consistent, you're setting the stage for ongoing success. After all, when those improvements roll in, you'll want to have solid data to back up your achievements and inform your next moves.

WRAPPING IT UP

Discipline in One Page

As we draw this final destination to a close, understand that the principles of continuous improvement, systems thinking, and the theory of constraints aren't only academic concepts.

Continuous improvement isn't about making grand, sweeping changes. It's about fostering a culture where every team member, from the c-suite to the front lines, continuously looks for ways to improve things. The production line worker suggests a minor change that saves seconds per unit, and the sales rep refines their pitch after each call. These small, incremental changes compound over time, improving efficiency, quality, and overall performance.

Systems thinking teaches us that no part of an organization exists in isolation. Interconnection links every decision, every process, and every team member, creating a complex web of cause and effect. The air traffic control team handles not only planes; they're part of a larger system involving weather patterns, airport operations, airline schedules, and countless other factors. In business, understanding these interconnections is crucial. For instance, a change in your supply chain affects not only inventory, it ripples through customer satisfaction, financial forecasts, and even employee morale.

The theory of constraints reminds us that every system has a bottleneck, no matter how well-oiled. This constraint limits its overall performance. In our air traffic control scenarios, it is the number of runways, the limitations of technology, the capacity of the airways, or the human capacity for handling stress. In your business, it is production capacity, market demand, or regulatory hurdles. The key is to identify these constraints and focus your improvement efforts there. Improving non-constraint areas feels productive but won't affect overall system performance.

Together, these three concepts form a powerful triad for driving business value. Continuous improvement provides momentum, systems thinking gives us the big picture, and the theory of constraints tells us where to focus our efforts for maximum impact.

As you leave this chapter, I challenge you to examine your organization through these lenses. Where are your opportunities for continuous improvement? How do the various parts of your business interact as a system? And most importantly, what's the constraint holding you back from reaching the next level of performance?

Standing still is not an option. Markets change, and new challenges emerge. The organizations that embrace these principles: improving, considering the complete system, and pushing against their constraints, will survive and thrive.

THE NEXT LEG OF YOUR FLIGHT BEGINS

The Start, Not the Finish

As we reach the end of this exploration into enterprise value creation, I hope that you feel energized and equipped to tackle the challenges. We've covered a lot of ground, from the intricacies of air traffic control to the nuances of organizational behavior. But more than merely a collection of concepts and case studies, this book is a roadmap for your journey of continuous improvement and strategic excellence.

Research and Evaluation, Strategy, Culture, Urgency, Execution, and Discipline, the RESCUED framework provides a holistic approach to business transformation. But remember, it's not a rigid formula to be followed blindly. Instead, it's a flexible guide that to be adapted to your unique circumstances.

Keep these principles in mind:

1. Start with an unvarnished understanding of your current state. Honest self-assessment is the foundation for meaningful change.

2. Strategy isn't grand visions - it's making tough choices and aligning your organization to execute them.

3. Culture is the lifeblood of any organization. Foster open dialogue and ensure that information flows in every direction. Give people purpose framed in non-negotiable values and driven by optimized processes.

4. Urgency is about creating momentum. Highlight the stakes, both the opportunities and risks, to ensure your team feels the need to act now. Identify critical priorities that will make the biggest impact and allocate resources accordingly. Set clear deadlines and expectations. Urgency

shouldn't create chaos—guide your team with clarity, resources, and encouragement to deliver their best work.

5. Execution is where strategies succeed or fail. Pay attention to the details, measure what matters, and be relentless in your pursuit of results.

6. Discipline turns onetime successes into sustained excellence. Create systems that reinforce continuous improvement.

Scotland has an iconic landmark: the Forth Rail Bridge, a fascinating design completed in 1890.

For much of its life, the famous rail crossing required a permanent team of workers to paint its entire structure from end to end continuously. In the early 20th century, it took a team of 50 men three years and 18 tons of paint to keep the 1890-built bridge corrosion-free and looking fresh, by which time the entire process had to be repeated. It was the very definition of a steady job.

The quirk became so well known that the phrase "painting the Forth Bridge" soon entered common parlance among Scots to describe any never-ending task.

The RESCUED method is like painting the bridge. Consider the process as never finished. You must adopt a mindset of continuous scanning and vigilance. Just as controllers monitor their radar screens for potential conflicts or opportunities to optimize traffic flow, you must consistently scan your business environment for areas of improvement and early signs of trouble.

This continuous scanning isn't a sign of paranoia or a lack of confidence. Instead, it's a recognition of the dynamic nature of business. Markets shift, technologies evolve, and new competitors emerge, often with surprising speed. By maintaining constant awareness, you position yourself to respond proactively rather than reactively.

Remember, every scan of your business "radar" is an opportunity. It reveals a process to be streamlined, emerging market trends you capitalize on, or a potential risk you mitigate before it becomes a crisis. This ongoing observation, analysis, and adjustment cycle separates excellent organizations from those that merely survive.

The business world, like the skies above us, is changing. New technologies emerge, customer preferences shift, and competitive landscapes evolve. But by embracing the principles we've discussed and committing to this perpetual process of improvement, you will confidently navigate this complexity.

As you close this book and return to your daily challenges, I encourage you to start small. Choose one area where you apply these concepts immediately. Perhaps it's mapping a process in your organization or re-evaluating your measurement systems to focus on leading indicators. Whatever you choose, take that first step.

Your journey toward excellence and operational mastery begins now. There will be turbulence along the way, unexpected obstacles to navigate, and moments of uncertainty. But armed with the insights and tools from this book, guided by your own experience and intuition, and committed to continuous scanning and improvement, you have everything you need to succeed.

From the Tower to the Boardroom

Final Reflections

Looking back, I realize my journey from the tower to the boardroom wasn't an accident. It was a natural evolution, a unique path that allowed me to bridge two worlds and bring nuanced learnings from one to the other.

I suspect that readers of this book are leaders who embrace continuous learning or aspire to lead. In the book "The CEO Test" (A must-read), Adam Bryant and Kevin Sharer discuss the challenges that make or break leaders.

They suggest leaders must be capable of:

1. Developing a simple strategy

2. Making the culture real and matter

3. Building teams

4. Leading transformation

5. Listening

6. Handling a crisis

7. Mastering the inner game of leadership

In writing this book, I give you the foundations to grow your leadership skills and succeed in the metric used to judge your abilities: value creation.

I say to the 'accidental strategists'-the former teachers now leading teams, the ex-athletes now running companies, and the artists turned entrepreneurs, embrace your unique journey. The perspectives you bring from your experiences are not liabilities but secret weapons.

I left the control tower but never the world of air traffic control. I'm still directing traffic, navigating complexity, and working to ensure safe and efficient operations. The aircraft have become companies; the radar screens are now spreadsheets and dashboards. However, the fundamental challenges—and the thrill of overcoming them—remain the same.

So, here's to the unexpected journeys, the accidental careers, and the surprising ways our experiences shape our future successes. May we continue to scan the horizons, adapt to changing conditions, and guide our charges in whatever multiverse we discover. With that, let me leave you with one more story, but this time from my days in the Merchant Navy.

Driving a Supertanker

The Perils of Momentum

You are leading a business that has gained momentum. Heed these words of caution.

As a navigation cadet, I was at the helm of a colossal supertanker on a rainy midnight to 4 a.m. watch. The Captain and harbor pilot were standing beside me. We were heading into port to offload our cargo of crude oil, picked up in the Middle East six weeks earlier.

A large ship, but one that was about $1/5^{th}$ our size, appeared out of the dark and rain. The ship was seemingly oblivious to our presence and on a collision course. Technically, the smaller ship had the right of way, given its position and direction of travel and as dictated by international maritime regulations. Still, there was a caveat to that rule; ultimately, both captains must take action to avoid a collision. The problem was that we weighed over 300,000 tonnes, were 1100 feet long, 176 feet wide, and had a draft of nearly 65 feet.

Turning was not an option in a narrow channel that was only a few feet deeper than our draft. With our size, we were also not stopping. We had too much momentum.

The other ship's captain had two choices: get out of the way or get run over. He chose violence and stopped his ship directly in front of us. An action so bad, it was never considered in our plans.

As the collision seemed imminent, my captain fell to his knees and started sobbing, thinking no doubt of the imminent end of his career and how to explain to the authorities why two hundred thousand tons of crude oil were polluting the river and destroying wildlife. A few moments later, when everything appeared lost, the second mate stationed on the fo'c'sle (the pointy end) reported that we had passed behind the other ship by only 5 feet.

What is the business lesson?

Suppose you are making waves in your industry. In that case, you will attract the attention of the competitive supertanker(s) who want a piece of your market. Scratch that; they want it all. They will run you over. They have the size and resources to make your life difficult.

Your own momentum can also be a hindrance. Like a supertanker, it is difficult to change direction. Momentum is the enemy of nimble.

Remember this tale as you create and assess your strategies and grow from ten to fifty million dollars and beyond. What do you do when the competition goes gloves off? Making your company valuable is one level of protection. Strategy, execution, and discipline are others.

Falling to your knees and sobbing is not.

APPENDIX A – THE ReSCUED STRATEGY MATRIX
Discovery Exploration at Work

Did you know that in a lottery where the jackpot winner picks only six numbers out of 49, the odds of winning the jackpot are approximately 1 in 13,983,816? Double the pick to 12 numbers; the odds have grown exponentially to 1 in 92,263,734,836. There is no need to check the math. The internet says it's correct.

As you embark upon your strategy exploration, you realize that the exploration produces so many insights that you feel overwhelmed. How do you sort and prioritize so much data? You end up with hundreds of data points across each of the steps.

To navigate this intricate decision-making landscape, leaders often employ a mix of analytical tools and intuitive judgment. Techniques like decision trees, simulation, and weighted scoring models help structure the problem and quantify trade-offs. Let's be honest; the more difficult this becomes, the less likely we are to follow through.

Earlier in this book, I claimed that air traffic controllers have one skill that stands above all others: we create clarity from complexity. In the last section, you will understand how to create a prioritized list of strategic initiatives and how that list becomes an evolving, dynamic guide for your organization.

This appendix will guide you through several stages of analysis and assessment, resulting in a list of ranked business differentiators and strategy initiatives, the starting point for the execution phase of value creation.

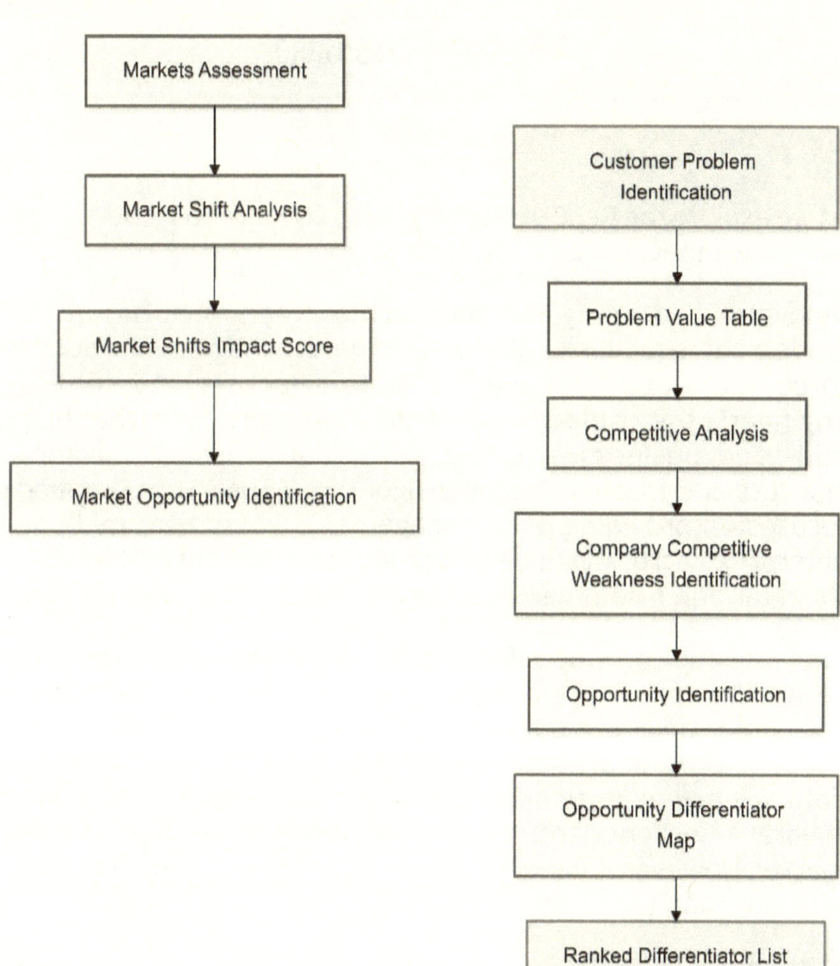

Meet InnovateX
A Fictional Use Case

As we explore the ReSCUED Scoring Matrix, we will use the fictional company InnovateX as a use case.

InnovateX is a young, dynamic tech company that has quickly made a name for itself in AI-powered data management. Founded three years ago by a team of data scientists and software engineers, the company has developed a platform that helps mid-sized businesses harness their data through advanced analytics and machine learning algorithms. Their current market focuses on providing data management solutions to mid-sized enterprises across various industries, with particular strength in the retail and e-commerce sectors.

The flagship product, DataSense AI, offers real-time data integration, predictive analytics, and customizable dashboards. The platform has gained traction for its user-friendly interface and ability to provide actionable insights without requiring extensive data science expertise from its users. InnovateX has secured several key clients and has seen steady growth in its existing market. However, it faces increasing competition from established tech giants and innovative startups.

As the business looks to expand and solidify its market position, it is exploring new market opportunities where its AI and data management expertise provide value. The company's leadership is particularly interested in markets that offer potential for recurring revenue streams and align with its mission of democratizing access to advanced data analytics tools.

Market Data Synthesis
Creating Commercial Insights

This is the first opportunity to explain the scoring matrix, which we will use throughout the exploration.

The scoring matrix will synthesize your findings, making it easier to determine the market approach most promising for your business.

As you read this appendix, understand that the chosen scores and weights are arbitrary. Your business priorities and peculiarities will drive the factors you choose.

Market Factors

Start by choosing several market factors you consider important in deciding which market to tackle. Example factors are:

Revenue Type: Non-recurring, Recurring, and Mixed

Growth Opportunity: Low, Medium, and High

Profit Potential: Low, Medium, and High

Market Risk: Low, Medium, and High

Cost to Enter Market (satisfying the must-haves): Low, Medium, and High

This is an arbitrary selection for demonstration. Your objectives will influence your business choices and how many factors to include.

Assign a score to each choice. I will use 1, 4, and 10, with the higher score being the most desirable, e.g., a recurring revenue market (10 points) is more desirable than a non-recurring revenue model

(1 point).

Important: The scores will be reversed if the factor is negative. The cost of entry detracts from the market appeal. If cost of entry is determined to be high, its score will be low.

Refine the scoring further by assigning a weight to factors influencing the impact on the total score. For example, if revenue type (weight 4) is more important in your market selection than profitability (Weight 2).

Existing Market Scores and Analysis

Factor	Score	Weighted Score
Revenue Type (Weight 4)	Mixed (5)	20
Growth (Weight 3)	Medium (5)	15
Profit (Weight 2)	Medium (5)	10
Market Risk (Weight 2)	Medium (5)	10
Cost of Entry (Weight 2)	Low (10)	20
Total		75

Market Shifts - Small Business AI-Powered Analytics

Existing Market Desirability Factor: 75/110 = 55%

Given your scoring criteria and weights, you have determined that the perfect market score is 110 points (The sum of the maximum weighted scores). The existing market scored 75 points, with a desirability factor of 75/110 = 68%.

Existing Market Analysis

1. Revenue Type: InnovateX's current market offers a mix of recurring revenue from subscriptions and onetime charges for implementation and customization. While this provides a steady income stream, there's potential to increase the recurring revenue portion.

2. Growth Opportunity: The market shows steady growth as more mid-sized enterprises recognize the need for advanced data management solutions. However, increasing competition between established players and new entrants limits explosive growth opportunities.

3. Profit Potential: The current profit margin is good, reflecting the high-value nature of AI-powered data solutions. However, increasing competition may put pressure on prices in the future, potentially affecting profitability.

4. Market Risk: The risk is medium. While the need for data management solutions is well-established, rapid technological advancements mean InnovateX must continuously innovate to maintain its market position.

5. Cost to Enter/Maintain: Already established in this market, the costs to maintain its position are relatively low. However, ongoing R&D investments are necessary to stay competitive.

The overall percentage desirability factor of 68% suggests that while InnovateX's current market is solid, there is room for improvement or expansion. This score provides a useful benchmark for evaluating potential new markets.

New Market Option A: Healthcare Data Analytics - Scores and Analysis

Factor	Score	Weighted Score
Revenue Type (Weight 4)	Recurring (10)	40
Growth (Weight 3)	High (10)	30
Profit (Weight 2)	High (10)	20
Market Risk (Weight 2)	Medium (5)	10
Cost of Entry (Weight 2)	High (1)	2
Total		102

New Market Option A: Healthcare Data Analytics

Option A: Healthcare Data Analytics Desirability Factor: 102/110 = 93%

Option A: Healthcare Data Analytics Analysis

This market shows high potential with a desirability factor of 93%. It offers recurring revenue, strong growth opportunities, and profit potential, which are advantages. However, the high cost of entry and medium market risk are notable drawbacks that need careful consideration. The healthcare industry's complex regulations and data privacy concerns contribute to the higher entry cost and risk.

New Market Option B: Small Business AI-Powered Analytics - Scores and Analysis

Factor	Score	Weighted Score
Revenue Type (Weight 4)	Recurring (10)	40
Growth (Weight 3)	Medium (5)	10
Profit (Weight 2)	Medium (5)	10
Market Risk (Weight 2)	Low (10)	20
Cost of Entry (Weight 2)	Low (10)*	20
Total		105

New Market Option B: Small Business AI-Powered Analytics

Option B: Small Business AI-Powered Analytics Desirability Factor: 105/110 = 95%

*Reversed Cost of Entry score as a low cost of entry is positive.

Option B Small Business AI-Powered Analytics - Analysis

This option scores a little higher than Market A, with a 95%

desirability factor. It also offers recurring revenue but with medium growth opportunity and profit potential. The lower risk and entry costs are advantages, making it an attractive option for more conservative growth or if InnovateX has limited resources for market entry. This market is less saturated and has fewer regulatory hurdles than healthcare.

These examples show how different factors balance each other in decision-making. While both markets score high, they present different opportunities and challenges. Market A, offers higher growth and profit potential, but higher risk and entry costs. Market B offers a more balanced approach with lower risk and entry costs but potentially lower growth and profit.

The choice between these markets depends on InnovateX's resources, risk tolerance, and long-term strategy. The healthcare market offers substantial long-term rewards but requires more initial investment. In contrast, the small business market provides a quicker and easier entry point for expansion.

Comparison of InnovateX Market Options

Desirability Scores

1. Existing Market (Mid-sized Enterprise Data Management): 68%

2. New Market Option A (Healthcare Data Analytics): 93%

3. New Market Option B (Small Business AI-Powered Analytics): 95%

Growth Opportunity

1. Existing Market: Medium (5): Weighted score 15 points

2. Healthcare Data Analytics: High (10): Weighted score 30 points

3. Small Business AI-Powered Analytics: Medium (5): Weighted score 15 points

The healthcare market shows higher growth potential than the existing market and the small business market. This suggests that healthcare data analytics offers InnovateX a more dynamic expansion opportunity.

Profit Potential

1. Existing Market: Medium (5): Weighted score 10 points

2. Healthcare Data Analytics: High (10): Weighted score 20 points

3. Small Business AI-Powered Analytics: Medium (5): Weighted score 10 points

The healthcare market again stands out with higher profit potential because of the high value placed on healthcare data and the complexity of the solutions required.

Market Risk

1. Existing Market: Medium (5) - Weighted score 10 points

2. Healthcare Data Analytics: Medium (5) - Weighted score 10 points

3. Small Business AI-Powered Analytics: Low (10) - Weighted score 20 points

The small business market presents lower risk compared to both the existing market and the healthcare market. This is attractive if InnovateX is looking for a safer expansion option.

Cost to Enter Assessment

1. Existing Market: Low (10): Weighted score 20 points

2. Healthcare Data Analytics: High (1): Weighted score 2 points

3. Small Business AI-Powered Analytics: Low (10): Weighted score 20 points

This shows one of the most significant differences. The healthcare market has a much higher cost of entry, likely because of regulatory compliance needs and the specialized knowledge required. The small business market, however, has a low cost of entry similar to InnovateX's existing market.

Revenue Type

1. Existing Market: Mixed (5): Weighted score 20 points

2. Healthcare Data Analytics: Recurring (10): Weighted score 40 points

3. Small Business AI-Powered Analytics: Recurring (10): Weighted score 40 points

Both new markets offer the potential for more consistent recurring revenue compared to the mixed revenue model of the existing market. This provides more stable and predictable income streams.

Key Takeaways

1. Both new markets offer higher overall desirability scores, suggesting potential for improvement over the current market position.

2. The healthcare market offers the highest growth and profit potential but has entry costs and risk

3. The small business market offers a balance of low risk and low entry cost, with the benefit of recurring revenue, but without the healthcare market's high growth and profit potential.

4. While scoring lower overall, the existing market benefits from InnovateX's established position and low maintenance costs.

This comparison suggests that, while both new markets offer attractive opportunities, they present different strategic choices. The healthcare market represents a high-risk, high-reward option;

the small business market offers a safer path to expansion with steady returns.

What did we achieve?

A preliminary, scored, and factored evaluation of existing and new market commercial viability.

The remaining parts of the strategy exploration are required for every market strategy you consider viable. Now is the time to discuss and decide the order of viability and complete the following sections for one market strategy at a time.

Mapping Future Market Shifts
Navigating the Unpredictable Landscape

A scoring matrix refines your understanding of future market shifts. This approach assigns numerical values to each factor. This section aims to identify and evaluate key trends and potential disruptions impacting InnovateX's business in both its current and prospective small business markets (Option B). By assessing these shifts' likelihood, timeframe, and potential business impact, we provide InnovateX with valuable insights to inform their decision-making.

The following analysis examines various factors, from technological advancements and changing customer demands to regulatory shifts and competitive dynamics. Our analysis scores each potential market shift based on its probability, expected timeline, and the magnitude of its potential impact on InnovateX's operations and market position.

Step 1: Identifying Potential Shifts

Think about the broader forces shaping your industry and adjacent industries. Look for trends and potential disruptions that impact your business.

Let's again consider InnovateX. They have determined to continue with their existing market, but consider New Market Option B a potential shift. What works today may not work tomorrow.

They identify the following potential market shifts:

Current Market

1. As businesses become more data-driven, the demand for real-time analytics capabilities will grow. This shift requires

substantial upgrades to InnovateX's existing platform.

2. By adopting edge computing, processing and analyzing data changes, potentially causing InnovateX to adapt its architecture for distributed data processing.

3. Stricter data privacy regulations need changes to data handling and processing methods, affecting InnovateX's platform and potentially creating new compliance-related features.

4. While still distant, quantum computing could revolutionize data processing capabilities, potentially rendering current algorithms obsolete.

New Market: Small Business Powered AI Analytics

1. As AI tools become more accessible, small businesses will increasingly seek AI-powered analytics solutions, expanding the market and potentially increasing competition.

2. Growing demand for seamless integration with popular e-commerce platforms opens new opportunities and requires development efforts.

3. Small businesses favor AI solutions tailored to their specific industries, requiring InnovateX to develop more specialized offerings.

4. The popularity of voice-activated interfaces for analytics among small businesses is rising, potentially requiring new interface designs and natural language processing capabilities.

Analysis

For the current market, the greatest shift is the increasing demand for real-time analytics and stricter data privacy regulations. These shifts are highly likely and majorly impact InnovateX's business. The rise of edge computing is a medium-term consideration. Quantum computing, though potentially revolutionary, is a more distant concern.

In the small business market, the democratization of AI tools is the most likely shift, closely followed by the need for integration with e-commerce platforms. These shifts present both opportunities and challenges for InnovateX. The trend towards industry-specific solutions is a medium-term consideration that shapes product development strategies.

Both markets show potential for change in the near to medium term. The current market requires more focus on enhancing real-time capabilities and ensuring robust data privacy measures. While potentially easier to enter, the small business market needs rapid adaptation to changing customer needs and expectations of AI accessibility and e-commerce integration.

These market shifts underscore the importance of flexibility in InnovateX's product development and business strategies, regardless of which market they prioritize.

Step 2: Assessing Likelihood, Timeframe, and Business Impact

Once you have a list of potential shifts, it's time to assign a likelihood and timeframe for each.

Likelihood - How likely is this shift to occur? Assign a score of:

- Probable: Highly likely, based on current trends and evidence

- Possible: A reasonable chance of happening, but with some uncertainty

- Plausible: Less likely, but a possibility to be considered

Timeframe - When is this shift likely to impact your business? Use the following categories:

- Less than 3 years: A near-term impact that requires immediate attention

- 3 to 5 years: Strategy development must consider a

medium-term impact

- Over 5 years: A long-term impact that influences your vision and direction

Business Impact – What is the potential impact on the business if this shift occurs? Business impact is determined by the risk of the shift making the company's current market position and differentiators obsolete. Consider a business holding a patent for solar panel technology licensed by every company that manufactures solar panels. What is the impact on the business from a breakthrough in wind energy power generation that makes solar panels obsolete?

- Major: This shift causes damage to our existing product and service offerings and our business model

- Medium: The shift will require the business to adapt, but it will provide advanced warning

- Low: Not impactful enough to require action. The impact will be resolvable in real time

Scoring Key

- Likelihood: Probable (5), Possible (3), Plausible (1)

- Timeframe: Less than 3 years (5), 3 to 5 years (3), More than 5 years (1)

- Business Impact: Major (5), Medium (3), Minor (1)

Total Score: Sum of Likelihood, time frame, and Business Impact scores

Example Scoring – Let's score the current and new markets.

Current Market: Mid-sized Enterprise Data Management Solutions

Increased Demand for Real-time Analytics

Likelihood: Probable (5)
Timeframe: Less than 3 years (5)
Business Impact: Major (5)
Total Score: 15

Rise of Edge Computing

Likelihood: Possible (3)
Timeframe: 3 to 5 years (3)
Business Impact: Medium (3)
Total Score: 9

Increased Regulatory Pressure on Data Privacy

Likelihood: Probable (5)
Timeframe: Less than 3 years (5)
Business Impact: Major (5)
Total Score: 15

Adoption of Quantum Computing

Likelihood: Plausible (1)
Timeframe: More than 5 years (1)
Business Impact: Major (5)
Total Score: 7

Market Shift	Likelihood	Timeframe	Business Impact	Total Score
Increased Demand for Real-time Analytics	Probable (5)	Less than 3 yrs (5)	Major(5)	15
Rise of Edge Computing	Possible (3)	3 to 5 years (3)	Medium (3)	9
Increased Regulatory Pressure on Data Privacy	Probable (5)	Less than 3 yrs (5)	Major (5)	15
Adoption of Quantum Computing	Plausible (1)	Over 5 yrs (1)	Major(5)	7

Market Shifts - Existing Mid-sized Enterprise Data Management

New Market: Small Business AI-Powered Analytics

Democratization of AI Tools

Likelihood: Probable (5)
Timeframe: Less than 3 years (5)
Business Impact: Major (5)
Total Score: 15

Integration with E-commerce Platforms

Likelihood: Probable (5)
Timeframe: Less than 3 years (5)
Business Impact: Medium (3)
Total Score: 13

Shift Towards Industry-Specific AI Solutions

Likelihood: Possible (3)
Timeframe: 3 to 5 years (3)
Business Impact: Major (5)
Total Score: 11

Rise of Voice-Activated Analytics

Likelihood: Plausible (1)
Timeframe: More than 5 years (1)
Business Impact: Medium (3)
Total Score: 5

Market Shift	Likelihood	Timeframe	Business Impact	Total Score
Democratization of AI Tools	Probable (5)	Less than 3 years (5)	Major (5)	15
Integration with E-commerce Platforms	Probable (5)	Less than 3 years (5)	Medium (3)	13
Shift Towards Industry-Specific AI Solutions	Possible (3)	3 to 5 years (3)	Major (5)	11
Rise of Voice-Activated Analytics	Plausible (1)	Over 5 yrs (1)	Medium (3)	5

Market Shifts - Small Business AI-Powered Analytics

Market Shifts Analysis Summary

1. Existing Market: The biggest shifts are the increasing demand for real-time analytics and stricter data privacy regulations, scoring 15. These represent near-term, high-impact changes that InnovateX needs to address promptly.

2. Small Business Market: The democratization of AI tools is the most impactful shift, scoring 15, followed closely by the need for e-commerce platform integration (13). These shifts suggest a rapidly evolving market with new opportunities and challenges.

3. Comparison: Both markets face near-term shifts that impact InnovateX's business. However, the small business market shows a slightly more diverse range of potential changes, which offers more opportunities for innovation and differentiation.

4. Long-term considerations: Quantum computing in the existing market and voice-activated analytics in the small business market are long-term considerations with lower overall scores. While potentially impactful, these are less urgent priorities.

You now have a clear, comparative view of the potential market shifts InnovateX faces in its existing and potential markets. They highlight the most pressing concerns and opportunities, helping to guide strategy and resource allocation.

Use a simple matrix to visualize and prioritize these potential shifts. You must create an additional matrix for each new market you are considering.

Strategic Implications of Market Shifts

The market shifts tables provide insights that inform InnovateX's future strategy decisions. By understanding potential changes in their existing and potential new markets, InnovateX proactively positions itself for success. Here's how these tables guide decision-making:

1. Prioritization of R&D Efforts: The high scores for Increasing Demand for Real-time Analytics in the existing market and Democratization of AI Tools in the small business market show areas where InnovateX will focus its R&D efforts. *Example*: InnovateX prioritizes enhancing its real-time analytics capabilities for its enterprise solutions while simultaneously developing more user-friendly, accessible AI tools for potential small business clients.

2. Resource Allocation: The tables highlight the most imminent and impactful market shifts, helping InnovateX allocate its resources effectively. *Example*: Given the high score and near-term timeframe for Increasing Regulatory Pressure on Data Privacy in the existing market, InnovateX needs to allocate resources to ensure compliance and develop robust data protection features.

3. Product Roadmap Development: The identified shifts directly inform InnovateX's product roadmap, ensuring that future developments align with market trends. *Example*: The Integration with E-commerce Platforms shift in the small business market suggests that InnovateX develop plug-ins or APIs for popular e-commerce platforms if they decide to enter this market.

4. Risk Management: InnovateX develops contingency plans and mitigates risks by identifying potential future shifts. *Example*: The "Rise of Edge Computing" in the existing market, while not imminent, suggests that InnovateX start exploring how to adapt its architecture for distributed data processing, preventing potential obsolescence.

5. Market Entry Timing: For the new market option, the tables help determine the optimal timing for market entry. *Example*: The high score and near-term timeframe for "Democratization of AI Tools" in the small business market suggest that if InnovateX enters this market, they do so sooner rather than later to capitalize on this trend.

6. Partnership and Acquisition Strategies: Identified shifts guide potential partnerships or acquisition decisions. *Example*: The "Shift Towards Industry-Specific AI Solutions" in the small business market prompts InnovateX to consider partnerships or acquisitions of companies with expertise in specific industries.

7. Competitive Positioning: Understanding these shifts helps InnovateX differentiate itself from competitors. *Example*: By preparing early for the "Rise of Voice-Activated Analytics" in the small business market, InnovateX positions itself as an innovator and gains a competitive edge.

8. Long-term Vision Setting: While some shifts are distant, they inform the company's long-term vision and aspirational goals. *Example*: While not imminent, the 'Adoption of Quantum Computing' shift suggests that InnovateX monitors this technology and considers how it will impact its offerings in the future.

InnovateX can maintain a dynamic, forward-looking strategy that adapts to changing market conditions by regularly updating and reviewing these market shift tables. This proactive approach will help ensure that InnovateX remains competitive and continues delivering value to its customers in its current market and any new markets it enters.

The Customer Value Table
It's Not What You Sell it's What Value You Provide

This exercise documents your understanding of the problems customers in those markets want to have solved. This exercise also assesses the severity of each problem, how valuable a solution to the problem is from your customer's perspective.

InnovateX. has developed a promising AI-powered platform for managing complex data, and the initial market response has been positive. You've even secured a few key clients. But as your company grows in your current market, you must differentiate yourself from the competition to succeed in a crowded market.

Step 1: Understanding the Problem

First, you must understand what problems your target customers face and how those problems translate into unmet needs.

In our InnovateX example, their target customers are mid-sized businesses struggling to manage and leverage large amounts of data. They have different pain points:

1. Data Overload: Businesses have bought a solution to the data storage problem. The abundance of data from multiple sources overwhelms them, making it difficult to sift through the noise and gain actionable insights.

2. Integration Challenges: Integrating diverse data sources and systems is a complex and time-consuming process, hindering the effective use of data.

3. Lack of Expertise: Businesses lack the expertise needed to implement and manage advanced data analysis tools, leading to inefficient utilization of their data assets.

4. Data Quality and Consistency: Organizations struggle with maintaining high-quality, consistent data across different systems and departments. Inconsistent or inaccurate data leads to flawed insights and poor decision-making.

5. Real-time Analytics Capabilities: Many businesses face difficulties in implementing real-time data analytics, which is increasingly crucial for making timely decisions in fast-paced markets. Existing systems often can't process and analyze data quickly enough to provide immediate insights.

6. Data Security and Compliance: With increasing regulatory pressures (such as GDPR, etc.) and growing cyber threats, companies find it challenging to ensure robust data security while maintaining compliance with various data protection regulations. This is especially complex when dealing with large volumes of data from diverse sources.

Value Analysis and Scoring

Now that you have identified issues where solutions add customer value, it is time to assign value scores.

1. Data Overload (High, 5): This remains a critical business issue. The ability to extract meaningful insights from vast amounts of data is crucial for competitive advantage and informed decision-making.

2. Integration Challenges (Medium, 3): While important, many businesses have managed this issue. However, it remains a pain point for some.

3. Lack of Expertise (Low, 1): This is still a concern, but with the increasing availability of user-friendly tools and training resources, it's becoming less of a critical issue for many businesses.

4. Data Quality and Consistency (High, 5): This is crucial, as poor data quality leads to flawed insights and decisions, potentially causing business impacts.

5. Real-time Analytics Capabilities (Medium, 3): While

important and growing in significance, not every business requires real-time analytics for their operations.

6. Data Security and Compliance (High, 5): With increasing regulatory pressures and cyber threats, this has become a top priority for businesses across industries.

Problem	Solution Perceived Value
Data Overload	High (5)
Integration Challenges	Medium (3)
Lack of Expertise	Low (1)
Data Quality and Consistency	High (5)
Real-Time Analytics	Medium (3)
Data Security & Compliance	High (5)

Customer Value Table for Data Management and Analytics

This table provides a snapshot of the relative importance of each problem from the customer's perspective. The high-value problems (Data Overload, Data Quality and Consistency, and Data Security and Compliance) represent areas where solutions provide value to customers. Medium-value problems are still important but are not as critical. The low-value problem, while still relevant, is not as pressing for most customers in the current market landscape.

If I asked you to choose which initiative to launch first, which would you choose? Data overload has a high value and is obvious. Sadly, it's not that simple. Does choosing three list items sum to a higher value than a single choice? Is that better than a single solution? Where are your competitors strong? What is the barrier and cost of entry for that problem solution? What is the timescale and risk in implementation? Let's keep investigating.

Step 2: Identifying Competitive Weaknesses

With a clear picture of your customer's needs, you can identify where your competitors are falling short. This is the key to finding your unique selling proposition.

Look for:

1. Limited Functionality - Are your competitors' platforms lacking specific features or functionalities that are valuable to your customers?

2. Integration Complexity - Are their solutions challenging to integrate with existing systems or technologies?

3. Limited Scalability - Can your competitors' platforms handle growing data volumes or evolving business needs?

4. Lack of Customization - Are your competitors' solutions inflexible and unable to be tailored to specific customer requirements?

5. Customer Experience - Do your competitors provide exceptional customer service?

6. Data Privacy Concerns - Do your competitors offer robust data privacy and security features?

Once more, let's present this information in an easier-to-distill format, the competitive strength matrix.

A further insight from this table comes from comparing your current or proposed solutions with the strongest competitor.

Competitive Weaknesses Table for Data Management and

Analytics Solutions

Explanation of Ratings:

- Weak = 1 point

- Satisfactory = 3 points

- Strong = 5 points

The problem's value multiplies each score (in parentheses) from the Customer Value Table.

Problem	Competitor A Solution	Competitor B Solution	Market Competition Factor
Data Overload (Value 5)	Weak = 1*5	Strong = 5*5	30/50 Points = 0.6
Integration Challenges (Value 3)	Satisfactory = 3*3	Weak = 1*3	12/30 Points = 0.4
Lack of Expertise (Value 1)	Strong = 5*1	Satisfactory = 3*1	8/10 Points = 0.8
Data Quality and Consistency (Value 5)	Satisfactory = 3*5	Weak = 1*5	20/50 Points = 0.4
Real-time Analytics (Value 3)	Weak = 1*3	Strong = 5*3	18/30 Points = 0.6
Data Security and Compliance (Value 5)	Strong = 5*5	Satisfactory = 3*5	40/50 Points = 0.8
Competitor Rating	62/110 Points = 0.56	66/110 Points = 0.60	

Competitive Strength Matrix

Competitor Analysis

1. Data Overload: Competitor B has a strong solution, while Competitor A is weak. There's room for improvement and differentiation here.

2. Integration Challenges: Both competitors have weaknesses, with Competitor A slightly better. This presents an opportunity for differentiation.

3. Lack of Expertise: Both competitors perform well, but it's also the lowest-value problem for customers.

4. Data Quality and Consistency: Neither competitor excels here, presenting an opportunity for differentiation in a high-value area.

5. Real-time Analytics Capabilities: Competitor B is strong, while Competitor A is weak. There's room for improvement to match or exceed Competitor B.

6. Data Security and Compliance: Both competitors perform well in this high-value area, with Competitor A slightly stronger.

Competitor B (0.60) performs slightly better than Competitor A (0.32) across these problem areas. However, there are obvious opportunities for differentiation, especially in high-value areas like Data Quality and Consistency and in addressing Integration Challenges.

The Market Competition Factor shows how well the market addresses each problem. Lower scores suggest areas where the market is underserved, presenting opportunities for an improved solution to gain a competitive advantage.

The next step is a critical self-analysis against competing solutions. This table compares InnovateX against the strongest competitor.

Problem	InnovateX Score	Competitor B Score
Data Overload (5)	Strong = 5*5	Strong = 5*5
Integration Challenges (3)	Satisfactory = 3*3	Weak = 1*3
Lack of Expertise (1)	Satisfactory = 3*1	Satisfactory = 3*1
Data Quality and Consistency (5)	Strong = 5*5	Weak = 1*5
Real-time Analytics (3)	Satisfactory = 3*3	Strong = 5*3
Data Security and Compliance (5)	Strong = 5*5	Satisfactory = 3*5
Total Score	96/110 Points = 0.87	66/110 Points = 0.60

InnovateX Self-Score Comparison Against Competitor B

Self-Score Competitive Analysis

1. Data Overload: Both InnovateX and Competitor B have strong solutions. This is a key area where InnovateX is matching the market leader.

2. Integration Challenges: InnovateX outperforms Competitor B. This is a strong differentiator for InnovateX.

3. Lack of Expertise: Both are satisfactory in this lower-value problem area.

4. Data Quality and Consistency: InnovateX has a strong solution where Competitor B is weak. This is another differentiator for InnovateX.

5. Real-time Analytics Capabilities: Competitor B has an edge here. This is an area where InnovateX could improve to match or exceed the competition.

6. Data Security and Compliance: InnovateX has a slight edge over Competitor B in this critical area.

Key Takeaways

1. Overall Position: InnovateX (0.87) outperforms Competitor B (0.60) across these problem areas. This suggests a strong market position for InnovateX.

2. Key Strengths: InnovateX's main differentiators are Integration Challenges, Data Quality, and Consistency. These are areas where InnovateX outperforms the competition.

3. Areas for Improvement: Real-time Analytics Capabilities are the only area where Competitor B outperforms InnovateX. This is a focus area for future development.

4. Maintaining Edge: In Data Overload and Data Security and Compliance, InnovateX matches or slightly exceeds Competitor B. Continued innovation in these areas will be important to maintain this competitive edge.

5. Low-Value Area: Both companies are equally satisfactory in addressing the Lack of Expertise. Given its low value to customers, this is not a priority area for further investment unless market demands change.

This comparison suggests InnovateX has a strong overall market position, with clear differentiators in key high-value areas. The improvement focus is enhancing Real-time Analytics Capabilities to match or exceed the competition.Maintaining the lead in other areas through continued innovation will be crucial for long-term success.

When evaluating your solutions, you must score higher than the strongest competitor's rating to be competitive and best positioned to win. In this overly simplistic analysis, you have an edge in the perceived value of your offerings at 0.86, but that is not the complete story. Where are you weak in the eyes of the customer? The fictitious company used for this examination has two areas for improvement: integration and expertise. The customer sees integration as more valuable, showing that this is an area where you will benefit from differentiation.

What did we achieve?

You have identified opportunities to apply differentiation to gain a competitive advantage. The assessment will impact the analysis of strategic initiatives in a later step.

VALUE AND DIFFERENTIATOR MAPPING
Ranking Differentiators

You have a potentially lengthy list of market problems at this stage. However, we have whittled that list down for our example.

Problem	InnovateX Self Score	Competitor B
Integration Challenges (3)	Satisfactory = 3*3	Weak = 3*1
Lack of Expertise (1)	Weak = 1*1	Weak = 1*1
Real-Time Analytics (3)	Satisfactory = 3*3	Strong = 3*5

Self-Score

Our opportunities for differentiation are in solving the Integration Challenges with a perceived customer value of 3 and the Lack of Expertise with a value of 1. InnovateX is weaker in real-time analytics when compared with competitor B. We need to address this. It makes sense to prioritize the one with the higher value. But is this the right choice? We need additional information; the analysis is incomplete.

For each problem, discuss the best differentiator and summarize how you plan to achieve it.

Problem	Differentiator Category	How (Strategic Initiative)	Strategic Importance
Integration Challenges (3)	Innovation	Develop an integration API that simplifies the integration with multiple sources of data.	High (5)
Lack of Expertise (1)	Exceptional Service and Community Building	Customer user group portal and 24/7/365 help desk.	Low (1)
Real-time Analytics Capabilities (3)	Innovation	Implement stream processing and in-memory computing technologies for real-time data analysis and visualization.	High (5)

InnovateX Differentiators and Strategic Initiatives Table

The strategic importance value measures how well the initiative attracts new customers, expanding current markets, or broadening the business by moving into new markets.

Analysis of InnovateX Strategic Initiatives

Problem 1: Integration Challenges

- Problem Customer Value (3)

- Differentiator Category: Innovation Strategic Initiative: Develop an API that simplifies the integration with multiple data sources.

- Strategic Importance: High (5)

Analysis

1. This initiative addresses a medium-value problem (3) but

has a high strategic importance (5).

2. The high strategic importance is justified because:

3. InnovateX already outperform Competitor B in this area, making it a key differentiator.

4. Effective data integration is crucial for deriving comprehensive insights, a core value proposition in data analytics.

5. Simplifying integration reduces client implementation time and costs, enhancing InnovateX's value proposition.

6. The innovation category suggests InnovateX aims to lead the market in this area, potentially creating a sustainable competitive advantage.

7. A well-designed API can become an industry standard, positioning InnovateX as a thought leader and potentially creating network effects.

8. This initiative also indirectly addresses the "Data Overload" problem by making it easier to merge and analyze data from multiple sources.

Problem 2: Lack of Expertise

- Problem Customer Value (1)

- Differentiator Category: Exceptional Service and Community Building Strategic Initiative: Customer user group portal and 24/7/365 help desk.

- Strategic Importance: Low (1)

Analysis

1. This initiative addresses a low-value problem (1) With a low strategic importance (1).

2. Despite the low ratings, this initiative serves several important purposes:

3. It addresses a common barrier to adopting advanced analytics tools.

4. It enhances customer satisfaction and loyalty, potentially reducing churn.

5. A strong user community is a valuable source of product feedback and ideas.

6. The 24/7/365 help desk, while resource-intensive, is a differentiator in the quality of customer support.

7. The user group portal fosters community among users, potentially increasing client switching costs.

8. While not a primary differentiator, powerful support and community features complement InnovateX's technical strengths, creating a more comprehensive value proposition.

Problem 3: Real-time Analytics Capabilities

- Problem Customer Value (3)

- Differentiator Category: Performance Enhancement Strategic Initiative: Implement stream processing and in-memory computing technologies for real-time data analysis and visualization.

- Strategic Importance: High (5)

Analysis

1. This initiative addresses a medium-value problem (3) has a high strategic importance (5)

2. The high importance is justified because:

3. It addresses an area where InnovateX currently lags Competitor B.

4. Real-time analytics are becoming increasingly crucial in many industries for timely decision-making.

5. Excelling in this area opens new market opportunities, particularly in sectors requiring immediate data insights.

6. The performance enhancement category suggests a focus on technological advancement, which aligns well with InnovateX's image as an innovative AI-powered platform.

7. Implementing stream processing and in-memory computing represent a technological investment, potentially creating barriers to entry for smaller competitors.

8. Success in this initiative positions InnovateX as a leader in high-performance, real-time analytics, attracting clients with demanding data processing needs.

9. This capability synergized well with the integration API, allowing for real-time data analysis from multiple sources.

Overall Strategic Implications

1. These initiatives show a balanced approach, addressing current strengths (integration), weaknesses (real-time analytics), and support needs (expertise gap).

2. A clear focus on technological innovation in high-value areas aligns with InnovateX's positioning as an AI-powered platform.

3. The initiatives create a comprehensive ecosystem: simplified integration, powerful real-time analysis, and strong user support.

4. Successfully implementing these initiatives differentiate InnovateX in the market, addressing key pain points while pushing the boundaries of what's possible in data analytics.

When prioritizing these initiatives, consider resource constraints, market demands, and potential synergies. The high strategic importance of the integration API and real-time analytics capabilities suggests these are a primary focus, with the support and community features as an important but secondary priority.

Prioritizing

Finally, we will rack and stack. For this, we will use four factors. The customer value score, the market shift score, the solution strength score, and the new strategic value score.

Problem	Customer Value	Market Shifts	Solution Strength	Strategic Importance	Score
Integration Challenges (3)	3 pts	3 pts	Strong (5)* Value (3) Total = 15	High (5)	26
Lack of Expertise (1)	1 point	5 pts	Strong (5)* Value (1) Total = 5	Low (1)	12
Real-time Analytics (3)	3 pts	5 pts	Satisfactory (3) * Value (3) Total = 9	High (5)	22

InnovateX Initiatives Scoring Table

Explanation of Real-time Analytics Scoring:

Let's break down the scoring for one problem, real-time analytics:

Customer Value 3 points: This aligns with the medium value (3) assigned in our earlier customer value table.

Market Shifts 5 points: We've assigned a high score here because real-time analytics are becoming increasingly important across various industries and align with the increasing demand for immediate insights.

Solution Strength 9 points: Satisfactory (3) * Customer Value (3) = 9. We've rated InnovateX's current solution as "Satisfactory" rather than "Strong" identifying as an area where InnovateX lags

Competitor B. The score of 9 reflects room for improvement in this area given the maximum score is 15 (value = 3, Solution Strength = 5).

Strategic Importance: High (5): This high score reflects the potential for real-time analytics to enhance InnovateX's competitive position and open up new market opportunities.

Total Score: 22

This puts real-time analytics between integration challenges and lack of expertise in priority.

Analysis of Table

1. Integration challenges remain the highest-scoring initiative, reinforcing its position as a key differentiator for InnovateX.

2. Real-time Analytics Capabilities now ranks second, highlighting its importance as an area for improvement and growth.

3. Lack of Expertise remains the lowest-scoring initiative, but its inclusion in the strategy recognizes the importance of comprehensive customer support.

4. The relatively close scores of Integration Challenges (26) and Real-time Analytics Capabilities (22) Suggest that both are top priorities for InnovateX, potentially pursued in parallel if resources allow.

This table provides a clear, data-driven prioritization of InnovateX's initiatives, balancing current strengths, areas for improvement, and market trends.

What did we achieve?

A ranked list of differentiators and initiatives that will drive the execution phase of your strategy and value creation.

Summary

Although our completed list was unusually short, the process has showed a way to make sense of the many data points you will uncover during strategy exploration. You have a picture of what markets are most viable, what customer problems are most valuable, and what approach to differentiation is like to create the greatest value in your business. Finally, you have a list of candidates for initiatives that will deliver the value you are driving for. Don't forget to go back and follow the Strategy Validation and Aligning the Organization Steps.